THE MONEY LAU

For a complete list of Management Books 2000 titles,
visit our web-site on http://www.mb2000.com

THE MONEY LAUNDERERS

Bob Blunden

2000

'There is no dirty money, there are only dirty people.'
Hans Keep, 10 June 1991

First published in 2001 by Management Books 2000 Ltd
Cowcombe House
Cowcombe Hill
Chalford
Gloucestershire GL6 8HP
Tel. 01285 760 722
Fax. 01285 760 708
E-mail: mb2000@compuserve.com

Printed and bound in Great Britain by Biddles, Guildford

British Library Cataloguing in Publication Data is available
ISBN 1-85252-367-0

Author's Preface

Years ago, I worked as a consultant with one of the world's leading fraud investigation consultancies. The founder and Chairman had a piece of advice given to all who would listen, which was, 'You have got to become seriously famous.' Whereas he already was famous (not, contrary to rumour, 'infamous'!), I had no aspirations or ambitions in that direction, because to become famous would mean that I would find it difficult to work undercover or slide off down to the pub – and who needs thousands of women begging to get to know you better?

However, I became embroiled in the fascinating world of money laundering and found that there were very few interesting books on the subject. There are a few manuals that tend to be dry tomes, excellent as reference guides or merely to look good in the office bookcase, to impress the visiting regulator that anti-money laundering is taken very seriously in this office. The few books that have been published tend to be case specific such as the infamous BCCI banking scandal or American publications with a bias to American cases.

No doubt you have noticed that money laundering articles appear weekly in the press and it's not just the serial criminals that are involved but everyone and their dog appears to have jumped on the bandwagon, from politicians (yes, I know – show me an honest politician), lawyers, accountants, and even good old Joe Bloggs selling counterfeit videos, CDs and smuggled cigarettes at the many car boot sales held in towns all over the country. They all need to hide their illegal income from the eyes of the authorities, whether it is political slush funds, bribes or cash from the sale of smuggled contraband.

It is interesting to discuss the problems of money laundering with those whose job it is to either prosecute, regulate or report such incidents. The law enforcement agencies tend to require justice to be granted with good criminal prosecution and appropriate punishment, whereas the financial institutions frequently seek the protection of the law by interpretation of those laws so that they are protected from criminal prosecution. In some ways, what money laundering really is and means has been forgotten by those who wish to interpret and follow the rules that suit them.

I suppose we all have been guilty of hiding that extra bit of income from the tax man – or the wife – but money laundering in the amounts of dirty money laundered by the serious criminal is a major problem that I fear will increase and go deeper underground to prevent detection, despite regulations.

Internet or cyber banking will, if unregulated, help the money launderer and, as this book goes to print, I read of a plan by a major telecommunications company to install thousands of ATM machines in pubs, clubs, motorway service areas and so on, throughout the United Kingdom, so that those without credit cards can deposit cash into the ATM and obtain a debit card electronically loaded with the cash value paid in. This card can then be used the same way as a credit card to purchase goods and services on the internet. When I asked the genius behind this idea how he was going to identify the source of the cash, the reply was *they would not be able to*. Needless to say, this means that the drug dealers will be able to deposit and convert their cash income, probably at the club or pub where they sold the drugs. The law enforcement agencies are not best pleased with this 'exciting' new business plan.

I hope that you enjoy the book, but whether I become seriously famous remains to be seen.

I would like to take this opportunity to thank Gordon Lewis, CIBC; John Riseborough, Standard Chartered Bank, Jersey; Det. Insp. David Minty, FCU, Jersey; John Gallachon, Jersey FSC; Andy Walker, Isle of Man FSC; Andy Turrell, FSA, London; Ed Wilding and Julian Parker of Maxima Group; Jon Walklin, BSB Ltd; and all who have advised and supported me in writing this book and helped in the fight against money laundering.

Bob Blunden
March 2001

6

Contents

Contents

'This fiver is definitely dirty.'

Introduction

I Would Like to Tell You a Story

Charlie West is a serious criminal and is also a respected businessman with a thriving antiques business in Yorkshire. Alan Jenkins is also a serious criminal and manages one of the North of England's leading casinos. Both manage an extensive drugs trafficking empire and both look like successful businessmen, dressing in conservative clothes with none of the ostentatious gold jewellery beloved of the nouveaux riches or the Arthur Daleys of this world.

It is mid-Sunday afternoon, that time of day in London's East End when the lunchtime pub-goers have returned home to the Sunday roast, some verbals from the wife and an afternoon's sleep in front of the television. The stall holders in the various street markets are packing up and street traffic is, for a change, relatively light and no longer represents the daily vision of one large carpark moving in one-yard jumps. A black Audi proceeds down the City Road towards Old Street. Charlie checks his watch, glances in the rear view mirror – the road behind is empty. 'Great,' he says, and turns into the one-way system at the top of Shoreditch. In the boot of the car are two cases containing two million pounds in cash.

Alan or 'Kosher' to his close friends, stretches his arms and rummages for a cigarette. 'So, we're almost there, Charlie?'

'Yep, we should have it all sorted within the hour – then we'll go up West – OK?'

The Spitalfields area of London has, in the profound wisdom of the local authority, been renamed Banglatown in recognition of the large Bangladeshi community. Curry emporiums, leather warehouses and Asian food stores stand cheek by jowl with a few remaining Jewish businesses, evidence of a previous influx of refugees from distant shores.

Small offices overlook the narrow streets where just over a hundred years ago Jack the Ripper stalked his unfortunate prey. In latter years, 'the Firm' held sway until the twins' incarceration and their subsequent death.

Charlie drives up Brick Lane and parks near the old Ind Coope brewery in Hanbury Street. Without digressing from this edge-of-the-seat story – the spot where Charlie parks is exactly outside where number 29 Hanbury Street stood until demolished for the brewery construction. This was the scene of the Ripper's murder of Annie Chapman, whose body was found dismembered in the back yard. Anyway, back to my story …

Charlie makes a quick call on his mobile phone, not being particularly concerned about the call being traced as the phone was one of the pay-as-you-go models, purchased for cash from Woolworths in Leeds, thus making the user completely anonymous. He ends the call, nods to Kosher and they get out of the car, remove the cases and quickly enter a door located between two Indian restaurants.

At the top of the narrow staircase, they open the door, enter a small room and are greeted by two Asian men who quickly check the contents of the cases. They are then ushered into the inner office where Rashmid Gautama quickly rises from his chair and greets Charlie with a firm handshake. 'It's good to see you again, Charlie.' He passes the torn half of a cinema ticket to Charlie who carefully places it in his wallet.

'OK, the usual 5% to you Rashmid?'

Rashmid nods and, after a farewell handshake, Charlie and Kosher give the car keys to Rashmid, leave the flat and walk west towards Liverpool Street station and a taxi to take them towards the bars and clubs of Soho, prior to their return north by train. The car had been rented, using false documents, from a national car hire group and is returned to a local franchise operator early the following day, the keys being deposited in a customer courtesy box as no staff are on duty to check the car in.

Rashmid quickly splits the money into numerous packages which are then taken by hand to various Asian businessmen operating Asian cash & carry and wholesale warehouses in the area, the cash soon being lost in a web of loans, cash income and creative accounting that even the best forensic accountant in the world would find difficult to unravel. Some of the cash will end up in legitimate bank accounts in High Street banks, being treated as business income.

Forty-eight hours later, in the Gold Souk in Dubai, a tall Australian walks into one of the many gold vendors and passes the torn half of the cinema ticket to a Pakistani sitting in a plush leather chair behind a large display counter. The vendor opens a drawer pulling out half of a cinema ticket and fits the two halves together – a perfect fit. He signals to an assistant who takes the ticket to a small office a few streets away. Later that day, gold is packaged and sent to the office where it is then sold to another vendor. The torn half of a playing card is then given to a courier who takes it in his wallet on a flight to Amsterdam.

The courier, mixing with the tourists in Amsterdam's red light district, bumps into a street vendor, passing the playing card to him. Later that night, the other half of the card is matched and within a few hours, drugs have been loaded onto a coaster heading for Humberside the following day, with a cargo of timber. The drugs are dropped off while the vessel is slowly heading up the River Ouse towards Goole, a crew member throwing the packages into some bushes on the riverbank. Two men, in a van parked in the small village of Blacktoft, watch the packages being thrown and quickly retrieve the drugs, loading them under several boxes of wet fish, purchased earlier at Kingston Upon Hull fish market. They then head for the M62, Leeds and Manchester. The drugs are for sale on the street only seven days after Charlie's visit to Rashmid.

Various 'dealers' collect the cash from the addicts and twice a week the funds are taken to a Casino in Leeds. Charlie likes a flutter and usually comes out on top with substantial cash winnings. The funds not 'won' by Charlie became part of the Casino's legitimate income. The Casino's profits are paid by dividends to shareholders every year. The main shareholder is a trust company set up several years previously in an offshore jurisdiction and administered by a local attorney. The dividends are invested in property, blue chip shares, bearer bonds and pension funds.

In the meantime, Charlie's antique business is doing quite well, and the manager of his bank is only too happy to check out Charlie's business plan with supporting accounts to extend a business loan for the new shop in Harrogate. Of course, antique dealers like dealing in cash, so each week, buyers acting for Charlie visit the various antique markets and centres buying some good pieces for cash, money that several hours previously had been taken from drug addicts in Manchester and Liverpool. Although some of the antiques are retained, the majority are sold back to the trade or to collectors through the auction rooms. Cheques from auction houses could be seen by the bank as legitimate funds, which, although declared in the annual accounts, are well worth the expense of tax and commissions.

Once a month, Charlie and Kosher go on a buying expedition to London where they invariably meet either Rashmid or his family and, once a month, drugs are smuggled into the United Kingdom to meet the demands of the Leeds/Manchester drugs market. Other drugs such as cocaine and cigarettes (a good, new lower-risk market due to the differential between UK and European prices) are sourced from other criminal organisations.

This 'story' (sorry – I'm no Ian Fleming, and the characters are fictitious) briefly outlines some of the methods by which the criminal will both launder his funds and hide them from the scrutiny of the authorities. In this particular case, the Asian hawallah system was used by the suppliers and other, more conventional money laundering schemes through the casino and antiques trade were used by Alan and Charlie. I would comment that the Asian/Chinese underground banking systems used by the Triads and Asian organised crime, are probably the most difficult in the world to unravel and investigate satisfactorily.

You may think that this story is a bit dated as, yet again, the drugs trade is used to illustrate money laundering. Unfortunately, the majority of dirty money still originates from that business. In this particular example, the drugs purchased were heroin, which you will read later is controlled by the Asian gangs – thus the hawallah secret banking system is more likely to be used. Of course, money obtained from other crimes will be laundered in different ways and this book details some of the methods used by the criminals to hide their funds, whatever the crime.

More about them later – but what is money laundering ?

Money Laundering

Recipe of Ingredients

Cash or valuables that are proceeds of criminal activity (criminal activity can be drug production and selling, smuggling, theft, blackmail, murder, terrorism, tax evasion and any crime, that if committed, results in financial gain)

Equipment required

- **Financial institutions:** (banks, investment advisors, lawyers, accountants, insurance companies or any facility that can process the profits of the criminal enterprise)

- **Company formation agents:** to provide off-the-shelf companies to use as a dressing to conceal the true taste, origin and colour of the money

- **Employees:** who are prepared to process the dirty money contrary to law and legislation

- **Computer:** to process electronic fund transfers through the anonymity of the internet

- **Regulatory Body:** that is either corrupt, ineffective, or lacking in statutory powers

Instructions

Find the most beneficial financial institution, deposit the funds using either a shell company, an alias, or a legitimate front individual or organisation. Let funds settle, then transfer through a sieve of individuals, organisations etc, mixing with legitimate business revenue. Invest final fund realisation into legitimate business or to fund further criminal enterprise. The better the mix the better the results.

Yes, this 'cooking' recipe is contrary to the usual concept of money laundering which is seen as a washing cycle to clean dirty money. But before you get into this book (and wash your hands afterwards), I believe that it is important to consider the main ingredients and equipment (the washing machine) needed in the money laundering process, as closing down and proper control of any of these main 'equipment' factors can ensure that the launderer goes elsewhere. Also I see that the FSA in London can mean two things, the Financial Services Authority or the Food Safety Agency, so 'recipes' are, perhaps quite relevant.

The proliferation of company formation agents is still a loophole that requires both review and legislation. Whereas I am all for free enterprise, the ease with which the dishonest can set up companies with fictitious directors, shareholders and so on in many jurisdictions is a major problem and headache when looking for the true, beneficial owners of an organisation.

1

How It Works

I have written this book so that it is an easy read (most of the time) which, I hope, should help you gain an understanding of the background, the danger signs, the legislation and consequences of the processing of dirty money. I believe that you will find the subject interesting and welcome your comments and questions.

The book has been written to alert you to what is now a highly topical subject with important ramifications to the financial status of the United Kingdom's Isle of Man, Gibraltar and Channel Islands financial markets.

The problems of money laundering are increasing every day with unholy alliances between the South American drug cartels, the Mafia, Russian organised crime and the Asian gangs, meaning that joint ventures in the sale of drugs, arms (including nuclear weapons) money laundering and murder are just the tip of a very big iceberg. The criminals have obviously taken lessons from the multinationals in their style of management, organisation and anti-competitive alliances thus achieving a highly organised, sophisticated and ruthlessly run operation. It is worth recalling that famous quote in The Godfather – 'It's not personal – it's just business.'

This multi-billion-pound business allows the organised crime 'executive managers' to bribe and recruit accountants, lawyers, bankers and employees within those organisations that can process the proceeds of their criminal activity. Awareness of this potential problem is essential as part of any organisation's compliance standards. Its no good having good controls and procedures if you have the proverbial rotten apple in the barrel. Later in the book, I have detailed the need to look beyond the obvious.

The ever increasing use of the internet means that e-money can be transferred anywhere in the world the touch of a button with the source unidentifiable. In addition, there is the old style criminal who still needs to convert the proceeds of crime to clean money. Recent press reports show that tobacco smuggling into the UK is now bigger business than drugs, with higher profits and less risk. Obviously, all of these 'profits' need to be banked and invested away from the gaze of the authorities.

In an ideal crime, the proceeds of that crime are hidden so that recovery by the loser is impossible and all evidence is hidden.

Even in the incident of murder, the perfect crime is where the killer hides the body or bodies from discovery. The body becomes a missing person if reported as such, or just disappears unannounced and unreported. The activities of Fred West in Gloucester where bodies were hidden in walls and under floors in his house was a prime example of hiding the evidence to conceal the crime. The concealment of cash is no different – the criminal wishes to hide the evidence – and in today's high speed financial market, it is easier to hide cash than a body.

I do not envy you the problem, but hope that the following chapters will alert you to what is happening and how a few simple controls and checks may keep the dirty money away from your business.

What is money laundering?

Money laundering is the procedure to conceal the origins of criminal proceeds so that they appear to have originated from legitimate sources. The individuals who complete this process are

- concealing true ownership and origin of criminal proceeds
- maintaining control of these funds
- changing the form of their ill gotten gains
- obscuring the movement of the funds

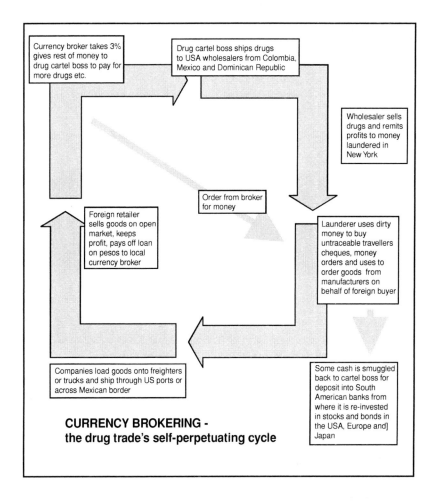

Currency broker takes 3% gives rest of money to drug cartel boss to pay for more drugs etc.

Drug cartel boss ships drugs to USA wholesalers from Colombia, Mexico and Dominican Republic

Wholesaler sells drugs and remits profits to money laundered in New York

Order from broker for money

Foreign retailer sells goods on open market, keeps profit, pays off loan on pesos to local currency broker

Launderer uses dirty money to buy untraceable travellers cheques, money orders and uses to order goods from manufacturers on behalf of foreign buyer

Companies load goods onto freighters or trucks and ship through US ports or across Mexican border

CURRENCY BROKERING -
the drug trade's self-perpetuating cycle

Some cash is smuggled back to cartel boss for deposit into South American banks from where it is re-invested in stocks and bonds in the USA, Europe and] Japan

Before the enactment of money laundering laws around the world, this concealment was easy as the various financial centres were only too happy to accept deposits of funds. One only has to look at the amount of money stolen by the Nazis and deposited in Switzerland to get the general idea. Whatever the changes in laws, the detrimental effect on a country's social fabric where money laundering occurs, has meant that the world map of where one can 'hide' funds is constantly changing.

The three stages of money laundering are universally recognised (in line with a washing machine cycle) as:

1. **Placement** (immersion)
2. **Layering** (heavy soaping)
3. **Integration** (spin drying)

1. Placement

This is the physical disposal of the criminal proceeds. The majority of such proceeds is cash which the criminal wishes to place in the financial system. In the case of drug revenue, this placement is needed to finance the business, whether that be to pay bribes, contract 'enforcers' or purchase transportation such as aircraft, boats, vehicles and so on.

Placement can include:

- depositing cash at a bank (often intermingled with clean funds to obscure any audit trail), and converting this cash to a readily recoverable debt
- physically moving cash between jurisdictions
- making loans in cash to businesses that appear to be legitimate or are connected to legitimate businesses
- purchasing high value goods for either personal use or as gifts
- purchasing the services of high value individuals
- purchasing negotiable assets in one off transactions
- placing cash in the client account of a professional intermediary.

A large proportion of the cash receipts from the US drugs market is used to buy merchandise from cash and carry warehouses which is then exported back to South America for resale by various 'retailers'. Jeffrey Robinson in his book, *The Merger* and recent press reports comment about the increase in Argentinean tourists to Paraguay, looking for duty free goods, and identify Ciudad del Este in that country as a centre for this type of trade, where visitors can buy anything at very reasonable prices.

This placement is also known as the immersion phase of the money laundering wash cycle. Originally, the money launderer would split the funds into small amounts below the $10,000 reportable sum and use 'couriers' to deposit these smaller amounts in various banks where counter-cheques or currency was obtained, then paid into dummy companies. This is called 'smurfing'.

Why smurfing? Well, you know those strange little blue men running around everywhere in Holland. The Dutch got so fed up with their takeover of the national culture, which, in my opinion was due to eating funny cakes in Amsterdam cafés, that they deported them to that melting pot of cultures, the good old USA. Here they gained employment running round banks depositing cash. If you believe that, I now know why you are reading this book!

One area that is excellent for placement is the antiques trade. Every day, a large number of people travel around the country visiting antique shops and auctions buying antiques for cash. So, say you have £100,000 to launder – it's simple. Check out the illustration overleaf.

Step One   Get a formation agent to set up a company so you have a name and a registered office address – cost £100.

Step Two   Drive around the country using the new company name to purchase antiques for cash. Let's say you have 10 pieces costing £5,000 each (total cost £50,000).

Step Three Split the stock between ten auction houses, ideally in ten different towns.

Step Four   Either let the pieces be sold to the highest bidder or use a 'friend' to buy the pieces back (using the £50,000 balance of your dirty money).

Step Five   The auction house receives £5,500 in cash for each piece (£5,000 hammer price plus 10% buyers commission). They send you a banker's draft for £4.500 (hammer price less seller's commission).

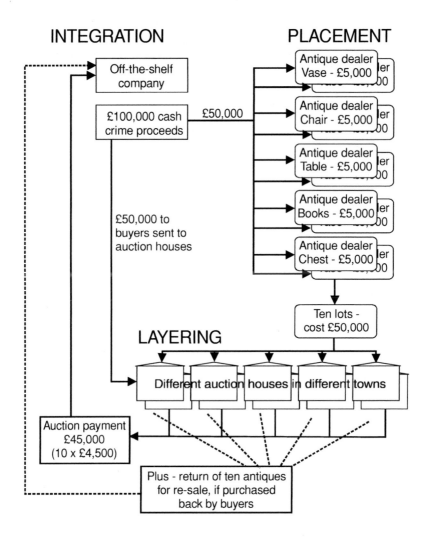

These are clean funds which you can bank as part of your new legitimate business, and you can sell the pieces again. These sales have cost you £10,000 which any criminal will accept as a reasonable expense of cleaning the money.

Auction houses, like expensive car dealers, are required to report suspicious transactions. The key word is 'suspicious'. As mentioned, hundreds of people buy antiques for cash at auctions and from antique dealers every day. Hardly any of these transactions are reported. Any business where cash is the normal method of payment such as fast-food outlets, video rental stores, casinos, bookmakers and so on are excellent venues for the placement of dirty money.

Another system is to tour the horse or greyhound racing tracks and purchase for cash winning tickets (obviously paying the punter a bonus) then claim the winnings backed up with a receipt. This is one of the latest schemes used by the criminal to launder drug money. Francis 'the Belgian' Vanverberghe, the mastermind behind the famous French Connection case, where drugs were shipped into New York from Marseilles concealed in a car, was recently murdered in Paris and evidence found on his body confirmed that he was operating such a scheme. This is yet another method for you to clean your dirty money.

2. Layering

This stage is where the money is separated from its criminal source by the creation of layers of transactions designed to disguise the audit trail and to give an appearance of legitimacy. Usually this is achieved by a wide variety of methods according to the opportunity given to, and the ingenuity of the criminals and their advisors. The layering stage is often called the heavy soaping stage.

Layering may include:

- rapid switches of funds between banks and/ or jurisdictions

- use of cash deposits as collateral security in support of legitimate transactions

- transferring cash through a network of legitimate and 'shell' companies across several jurisdictions (see Bank of New York case in Chapter Two)

- resale of goods/assets.

The Brinks-Mat gold bullion robbery and the subsequent laundering of the cash proceeds is an excellent example of layering. I shall detail the sequel of events in respect of that case in Chapter Two.

3. Integration

The final part of the wash cycle is the integration of the criminal funds as being legitimate, having been successfully immersed and layered. This stage is sometimes called the Spin Dry cycle. The proceeds are integrated back into the economy in such a way as they appear to be legitimate. The antiques example shows the three stages with the integration of the banker's drafts received from the auctioneers.

Examples of activities at the integration stage include:

- **false or inflated invoices** – paying inflated or deflated invoices for exports/imports provides an effective way to integrate the proceeds of crime in and out of an economy (this is a favourite ploy of the Russian crime syndicates). For example, exports to Japan from Russia have been deliberately under-invoiced by Russian businesses. Fish exports to Japan in 1994 were, according to Russian records, some 7,000 tonnes valued at $90.4 million whereas the Japanese claim imports to the value of 56,000 tonnes or $ 622 million. During the same period, crab exports were similarly under-invoiced by some $537 million. Something fishy was obviously going on.

- **Real estate** – criminals use a shell company to purchase property then sell the company with its assets for a 'legal' profit (used by the Brinks-Mat robbers to launder some of the proceeds of the sale of the stolen gold bullion).

- **Front companies** – the corporate secrecy laws in some countries permit the formation and operation of companies that do not reveal their true owners, only names of nominee directors. These companies, operated by criminals, lend themselves their dirty money in an apparently legitimate transaction and pay themselves 'interest' on the 'loan'. The interest can be treated as a business expense for tax purposes with a reduction in tax liability.

- **Foreign bank complicity** – hinders detection because it conceals activity relating to money transfers. With the assistance of corrupt bank officials, dirty money is used as security against legitimate loans. Bank secrecy laws make the chances of detecting such loans minimal. (Liechtenstein's financial businesses are under investigation for this type of activity.)

Some banks in Russia have made loans to dummy companies who subsequently invest the money in offshore companies controlled by the same bank. The dummy company defaults in repayment of the loan and the offshore company channels the money through more banks so as to obscure the origin. The promissory notes of the defaulting company are assigned to a third company who allow the lending bank to write off the original loan. This type of scam is also prevalent in Africa and I remember during an investigation into money laundering by an Indian hawallah dealer, discovering 'loans' amounting to millions of pounds to various 'companies' for construction of bottling plants and so on. Every 'loan' was subsequently written off.

Effect on Financial Centres

At the end of the last century, the proceeds of crime had grown tremendously. Whereas earlier in the 20th century, headline news was provided by the incidence of large crimes such as the Great Train Robbery, the French sewer bank robberies, the Knightsbridge safe deposit box heist and more recently, the failed Millennium Dome jewel heist ('I was only here for de Beers'), the growth of organised crime, especially in the drug trade, provided the organised crime syndicates with income beyond their wildest dreams.

This organised crime business, although the subject of various books and government reports, has to a degree been seen as part of the society that we live in. Only when a criminal is convicted are the public aware of the extent of the crime and possible money laundering.

Some sources put the dirty money income as $1 trillion dollars worldwide and that some 300 billion US dollars are currently circling the globe. The drug trade obviously has serious effects on a country's social fabric, with increases in crime to support drug habits, increase in AIDS and other health matters associated with drug usage and all that this means to the health and crime enforcement budgets of a nation.

In financially bereft countries such as Russia, where a large percentage of the nation's wealth and business is in the hands of criminals, the whole economy is on the brink of collapse unless the Government take appropriate action. The problem is that there appears to be evidence that friends and family of some of the senior politicians in Russia have accepted bribes and transferred 'funds' out of Russia.

When a financial centre is seen to be an easy conduit for dirty money, two things happen.

- the criminals, whether they be robbers, fraudsters, drug barons or despots, will be attracted like flies to a jampot, and this will result in …

- the World Powers, i.e. the USA and EC plus international bodies such as the United Nations, World Bank and so on, will attempt to close these financial centres down.

Obviously, a financial centre likes to pride itself on integrity, customer/client confidence and as an attractive place to invest funds. In other words – **a centre of financial excellence**. Therefore any incident of 'crime' involving a financial business within a financial centre, especially where the involved business is seen to have acted in a naive manner, brings unwanted publicity to the centre of excellence. Closure of a business or financial centre is going to cause unemployment and a drain on the local economy. The Barings Bank debacle not only embarrassed the City of London but caused the bank to collapse with subsequent unemployment and economic issues.

The need to ensure that the financial centres do not become the proverbial jam pots or, in money-laundering terminology, 'sinks', has resulted in a range of regulations and legislation. The lack of adherence to the law and regulations by some financial businesses has made the UK an ideal place to hide or launder money.

The recent German intelligence report (detailed in the following section) shows that Liechtenstein is under pressure to either clean up or close down as a financial centre. Panama was actually invaded by the US military because it had become a money laundering/drug trafficking centre.

As you may have read recently, the current investigation into what appears to be America's biggest money laundering scandal has highlighted the fact that London-based financiers, Lucy Edwards and Peter Berlin are in serious danger of assassination by Russian criminals to prevent them giving evidence about how they laundered some $8 billion through their bank accounts and companies.

The current fear is that Britain is facing an explosion of 'red mafia' crime (*Sunday Times*, 20 Feb 2000) and that London is already a money laundering haven (or sink) for East European gangs. Some £20 billion is estimated to be flowing through City coffers each year.

It is also expected that a further £25 billion will come into the UK from Switzerland as that country tightens its banking laws. Some 90 Swiss companies are known to be front operations for Russian criminals.

The National Criminal Intelligence Service (NCIS) confirm that the attitude of financial institutions in Britain must change. They reported in July 2000 that the increase in the reporting of suspicious transactions by financial institutions has increased dramatically in the last year.

However, there is still an increasing concern that the number of suspicious transaction reports that originate from solicitors and accountants remains low and it is believed that organised crime are using the strict client confidentiality rules of British lawyers and accountants to launder dirty money. In fact, at this time, six large law firms, suspected of laundering drug cartel money, are being investigated.

Recently I held two series of money laundering and fraud conferences in the Channel Islands and the Isle of Man. Following up the mail shot showed that, whereas the response from bankers and fund managers was excellent, the normal response from the majority of accountancy firms (especially the major international accountants) was 'we know all there is to know about money laundering.'

In other words, you cannot teach us anything new. I believe that this arrogance is one of the major factors behind the lack of the reporting by accountants of suspicious transactions in respect of client accounts.

I understand that the Financial Services Agencies in London, The Isle of Man, Gibraltar and the Channel Islands are taking a very pro-active stance to ensure that financial companies adhere to the law and regulations for the processing of money, and the FSA in London has now taken on responsibility for enforcement of the various UK financial regulations that in the past have been the administered by other agencies.

Sources of dirty money including areas of high risk

The main source of dirty money is from the world-wide drug trade originating in Central America and the Far East. This is followed by the influx of criminal profits from the old Soviet bloc, embezzlement by various despots in Africa and the old Soviet bloc, the illegal diamond trade, exchange control violations and the proceeds of any crime.

The problem is how can you be expected to identify that the cash deposit, wire transfer or whatever is the proceeds of crime?

It would be great if the new client entering your business speaks Spanish or Russian, wears dark glasses, lots of gold jewellery, smokes a large cigar and makes you an offer that you cannot refuse. Easy – he is obviously a crook and you can send him on his way. Unfortunately its not that simple. The drug barons have had years of practice in the art of money laundering and have set up systems so complex one needs to be an Einstein to unravel the web of transactions to identify the true source and beneficiary of the funds. So the source is invariably hidden and you are not going to see a transaction from a Colombian or Russian Bank.

Money laundering is about 'sleight of hand'. One author likened it to a magic trick for wealth creation and is the closest anyone has come to alchemy.

Al Capone and Bugsy Moran used coin-operated laundromats to disguise revenue from gambling, prostitution, racketeering and violation of the Prohibition laws and many claim that this is where the term 'money laundering' originated. This is wrong – the term perfectly describes the cycle of transactions that the dirty money passes through so that it comes out clean at the other end.

'It's not our business to inquire into our clients' morals.'
Hong Kong banker

So the sources of dirty money are world wide as crime is a multinational business – only the ice-caps are relatively clean. However, a large number of countries have not signed the International Agreements in respect of Money Laundering, so transactions from financial institutions in those countries must be examined closely.

These countries, and some that have signed agreements, but are continuing to accept dirty money, are known as 'sinks'. Currently these countries are:

- the various states within what was Yugoslavia, Pakistan, Hungary, Russia, Czechoslovakia, Bulgaria, Belize, Poland, Hong Kong, Liechtenstein, Luxembourg, Andorra, Switzerland, Singapore, United Arab Emirates, Bahamas, Cayman Islands, Mexico, Panama, and recently, various Pacific Islands.

- Some cities are also in this league of laundrymen – London, New York, Los Angeles, Miami, Houston, Montreal, Toronto, Vancouver, Macao and Hong Kong, to name just a few.

CROOKS TOURS
Summer 2001 Brochure
Holiday destinations to mix business and pleasure

Destinations are liable to change at short notice with new additions frequently

Bahamas - Cayman Islands - Cook Island - Dominica - Israel - Lebanon - Liechtenstein - Marshall Islands - Nauru - Niue - Panama - Philippines - Russia - St Kitts and Nevis - St Vincent and the Grenadines

- 15 jurisdictions have been identified in the recent (22 June 2000) Financial Action Task Force Report (see Chapter 2) as being non-cooperative in the implementation of anti-money laundering measures.

A recent German Federal Intelligence Service report (Bundesnachrichtendienst) alleged that currently Liechtenstein is the world's biggest money laundering centre. The report alleges that senior Mafia, South American drug barons and Russian underworld chiefs have been targeted by financial managers and politicians in Liechtenstein as desirable clients with the offer of secretive financial arrangements. The information was obtained by GFIS cyberspys who, using surveillance to tap into satellite and telephone communications, obtained intelligence to support the allegations.

The current scandal involving ex-Chancellor Kohl and illegal political party funding has identified that some of the funds were laundered through accounts in Liechtenstein. Evidence obtained by the Metropolitan Police identified that the proceeds of the Brinks-Mat gold bullion robbery were laundered through bank accounts in Liechtenstein. Serious allegations were made to the ruling Prince some three years ago about serious financial crimes in the principality involving senior financial officials, yet the letter was only allegedly passed to the Prince a few months ago.

Der Spiegel (the German newspaper) states:

'The secret document reads like the worst nightmare: an entire country, in the middle of Europe, appears to be in the service of criminals from all round he world. The findings destroy once and for all what was left of Liechtenstein's battered reputation.'

No doubt the European Union and other G-7 members will be pressurising this small principality to get its house in order. Despite denials in the press and during radio/television interviews, a special investigation team has now been called in by the Government. To date, several people, including bank officials and a politician have been arrested on suspicion of money laundering for Mafia and Colombian criminals. The Vaduz government has also introduced new legislation to fight money laundering with an emphasis on 'know your client'. Still, that will not worry the money launderers – there are plenty of other places to go.

A new and great place to launder money is a chunk of coral called The Republic of Niue. This atoll, some 2,400 miles North East of New Zealand, has been described by a senior law enforcement officer in Hong Kong as:

' Bird shit, telephone sex and money laundering.'

With a population of 1800, birds were there first, then telephone sex imported by the Japanese taking advantage of technology and the international telephone system (the local phone company receiving a share of the horrendous fees charged to the mug at the end of the line), followed by internet domain names, internet gambling and the cream on the cake, the world of offshore shell companies.

31

Since 1994, Niue has been licensing International Business Corporations (IBCs) which for $1,000 start-up fee gives anyone the right to incorporate a company in any language. IBCs are permitted to use any suffix that any company anywhere in the rest of the world can use such as Ltd, Inc, GmbH, SA, NV, whether they have business in those countries or not. It is impossible from the company's name to decipher what it does, or where it does it. It allows the company to pretend that it does something that it doesn't, and is somewhere where it isn't.

No minimum share capital is required and an IBC is exempt from local tax and stamp duties. There is no requirement to file annual accounts or hold general meetings. In addition, to maximise security of assets, they are permitted to transfer, domicile, re-acquire and re-issue shares for cash in any currency, or for any form of consideration. The shares can be bearer or nominative and to really complete the web, they can list other companies as directors so that it is impossible to find out who actually owns the company.

The latest offer is the facility to purchase banking licences. For under £20,000 one can have your very own financial institution. The sales brochures claim that it 'Provides access to the international credit market, as well as the international mutual funds market and securities market. It allows the bank to conduct FOREX transactions and, with minimal expense, solve the problems of liquidity.'

Formation Agents in London and on the web offer IBC formation and banks for sale with branch offices in Moscow and St Petersburg. It is believed that Russian businessmen have purchased several thousand IBCs and banks registered in Niue.

The Russian crime syndicates also use any other jurisdiction where money laundering controls are either nonexistent or weak. Cyprus is allegedly used to launder $1 billion per month and Russians have formed some 8,000 shell companies in that jurisdiction. However, that situation may change with the recent withdrawal of Beogradska Bank's banking licence (this bank is owned by Slobodan Milosevic who allegedly has links with the Mafia and has laundered money out of Yugoslavia to China and other locations). The Central Bank in Cyprus has revoked some 950 licences.

The Russians have also met Colombian drug cartels and Italian Mafia in the Caribbean where there are some 450 banks (many with no offices) registered in the Cayman Islands, and some three dozen banks have been registered in Antigua in the last few years, including at least four Russian owned and one Ukrainian bank (usually no more than an office with a computer).

The European Union Bank, chartered in Antigua, offers internet banking with all of the money laundering facilities that type of operation can facilitate. Israel, a jurisdiction with no money laundering laws, is also used to launder money with another $1 billion going through that country each month.

Companies in Russia only have to produce documents showing that they are importing something and they can transfer funds out of the country. These documents are usually false. Great Britain is a popular destination and the money has been washed in the City of London, sheltered in the Channel Islands and spent on property.

The French Government are currently lambasting Monaco as being a money launderers' haven. This is being strongly refuted by the principality, but with the casino and an influx of Russian 'businessmen', it is likely that this is true. The principality has 49 banks and 70 financial businesses with a population of 32,000 people and 320,000 bank accounts. The Aeroflot flight from Moscow to Nice is one of the airline's busiest, although many of the rich Russians prefer to use private jets. The journalist Roger Louis Bianchi, author of the book *An Affair that Turned,* an investigative book about the principality, claims, 'It is a factory of false accounting'.

Malta is also under the proverbial microscope and there has been evidence that Maltese companies have been front operations for the Libyan Government and alleged 'terrorist' operations.

However one must also question political motives and agendas in the identification of money-laundering suspect jurisdictions. Spain is not mentioned, yet criminals appear to easily invest their ill-gotten gains in the Costa Del Sol. Similarly, the jurisdictions that make up South America are cash-based economies which are ideal for the money launderer. Rarely does one read of money laundering problems in those jurisdictions – I wonder why?

Indications and tell-tale signs

The main vulnerabilities of money laundering are the following identified points:

- cross-border flows of cash
- entry of cash into the financial system
- transfers within and from the financial system
- acquisition of investments and other assets
- incorporation of companies and formation of trusts.

According to the Bureau for International Narcotics and Law Enforcement Affairs, US Department of State, Washington DC, the following criteria are used by drug money managers for the laundering of their drugs sales revenue:

- failure to criminalise money laundering from all serious crimes or limiting the offence to narrow predicates such as prior conviction of a drug trafficking offence

- rigid bank secrecy rules that cannot be penetrated for authorised law enforcement investigations or that prohibit or inhibit large value and/or suspicious or unusual transaction reporting by both banks and non-bank financial institutions

- lack of adequate 'know your client' requirements to conduct financial transactions or allowed use of anonymous, nominee, numbered or trustee accounts

- no requirement to disclose the beneficial owner of an account or the true beneficiary of a transaction

- lack of effective monitoring of cross-border currency movements

- no reporting requirements for large cash transactions

- no requirement to maintain financial records over a specific period of time

- no mandatory requirement to report suspicious transactions or a pattern of inconsistent reporting under a voluntary system; lack of uniform guidelines from which to identify suspicious transactions

- use of bearer payable monetary instruments

- well established non-bank financial systems, especially where regulation, supervision, and monitoring are lax

- patterns of evasion of exchange controls by nominally legitimate businesses

- ease of incorporation, especially where ownership can be held through nominees or bearer shares, or where off-the-shelf corporations can be acquired

- no central reporting unit for receiving, analysing and disseminating to the competent authorities large value, suspicious or unusual transaction financial information that might identify possible money laundering activity

- limited or weak bank regulatory controls, or failure to adopt or adhere to the Basle Principles for International Banking Supervision, especially in jurisdictions where the monetary or bank supervisory authority is understaffed, underskilled or uncommitted

- well established offshore financial centres or tax haven banking systems, especially jurisdictions where such banks and accounts can be readily established with minimal background investigations

- extensive foreign banking operations, especially where there insignificant wire transfer activity or multiple branches of foreign banks, or limited audit authority over foreign-owned banks or institutions

- limited asset seizure or confiscation capability

- limited narcotics and money laundering enforcement and investigative capabilities

- jurisdictions where there are Free Trade Zones where there is little government presence or other supervisory authority

- patterns of official corruption or a laissez-faire attitude toward the business and banking communities

- jurisdictions where the US dollar is readily accepted, especially jurisdictions where banks and other financial institutions allow dollar deposits

- well established access to international bullion trading centres in New York, Istanbul, Zurich, Dubai and Mumbai

- jurisdictions where there is a significant trade in or export of gems, particularly diamonds

- jurisdictions with large parallel or black market economies

- limited or no ability to share financial information with foreign law enforcement.

So how does your organisation measure up? Would it be possible to launder money through your company?

Vigilance

Although the regulatory bodies do not wish you to become detectives, there is a need and requirement to maintain vigilance so as to deter criminals from using your business for the purpose of money laundering. The task of detecting crime remains with the various law enforcement agencies, and your task is to maintain a duty of vigilance to avoid assisting the process of money laundering and to react appropriately should such an attempt be made. However, the regulatory bodies are making you self-policing and I think you can be likened to 'special constables'.

Most regulatory bodies see that vigilance encompasses the following control elements:

- verification
- recognition of suspicious customer transactions
- reporting of suspicion
- keeping of records
- training.

The regulatory bodies also recommend that a financial service business can perform their duty of vigilance by having systems that enable them to:

- determine (or receive confirmation of) the true identity of customers requesting their services

- recognise and report suspicious transactions to the appropriate regulatory body

- keep records for a prescribed length of time

- train key staff

- liaise closely with the appropriate regulatory body on matters concerning vigilance policy and systems

- ensure that internal audit and compliance staff regularly monitor the implementation and operation of vigilance systems

- ensure that all staff (new, temporary and existing) are subject of pro-active vetting

... and that you should not enter into a business relationship or complete a significant one-off transaction unless the above mentioned systems have been fully implemented.

Obviously the scale of these systems will depend on the size of the business but whatever the size the systems have to meet the standards set by the regulatory body.

The legislation usually calls for the appointment of a Reporting Officer and/or a Prevention Officer. Obviously the size of your business may necessitate combining the responsibilities.

Whatever the size of your business, the duty of vigilance begins with the start of the business relationship or a significant one-off transaction and continues until either comes to an end. However the keeping of records continues as a responsibility.

It is very important to note that:

all key staff are at risk of being or becoming involved in criminal activity if they are negligent in their duty of vigilance. They should be aware that they face criminal prosecution if they commit any of the offences which we shall detail in Chapter Four.

When employees move on to new employment within the financial services business, they may find a customer from their previous employment who had been the subject of suspicion and they have a duty to report such matters to their new employer.

We have discussed the effect on financial centres earlier, but the lack of duty of vigilance has a number of serious consequences. These can be summarised as:

- commercial failure by losing one's good market name, position and the incurring of non-productive costs and expenses

- the possibility of the regulatory body raising concerns in respect of the business being a fit and proper financial operation

- the risk of criminal prosecution and heavy financial and/or custodial penalties

- the risk to the employee of losing one's reputation, and criminal prosecution.

When the duty of vigilance is examined in relation to the legislation, it is important to note that two of the relevant offences are concerned with assistance given to the criminal. There are two aspects to such assistance:

1. the provision of opportunity to obtain, disguise, convert, transfer, conceal, retain or invest criminal proceeds; and

2. the knowledge or suspicion on reasonable grounds (actual or, in some cases, imputed if the person should have had a suspicion) of the person assisting that they are dealing with the proceeds of criminal conduct.

Involvement is avoidable on proof that knowledge or suspicion was reported to the regulatory body in accordance with the vigilance policy of your business. While prompt reporting removes the criminality from assistance, it is important to note that:

- any reporting which prejudices an investigation by either tip off or leak may constitute an offence

- any failure to report knowledge or suspicion may also constitute an offence.

Know your client(s)

This is without doubt the most important defence against the money launderer. A few years ago, I carried out a review of non-resident Indian clients for an American Bank based in London. The bank were concerned that some of their clients may have been involved in the Bombay Stock Exchange Fraud where millions of dollars were lost and disappeared. I found that the checks completed by the bank on these clients was so minimal that they may as well not bothered. Many had given residential addresses which I found to be rented accommodation where the clients had resided for a few days.

One client had a corner shop in a small town in Sierra Leone (probably the poorest country in the world) yet he had deposited nearly $3 million. No accounts had been provided to support the deposits and there was a reasonable opinion that the money came from illegal diamond smuggling (which is rife in Sierra Leone). There were many similar examples where examination of the client assets showed there were doubts about the origin of the funds. If the bank had completed properly designated background checks, many of the clients would not have been accepted and the risk of censure by the Bank of England eliminated.

A recent check I completed for a stockbroker on a potential client revealed that his residential address was an office rented to a company whose registered office was a semi-detached house in South London. His massive investment company registered in Jersey had a share capital of £2 with no published accounts and his other Jersey company had been struck off two years previously.

When asked about eight years that were missing from his CV, which he claimed had been spent rebuilding a $18 million chateau in the South of France, he admitted that he had been arrested by the French police and held in custody for 10 months for suspected money laundering. If he was as rich as he claimed, why did he spend all of that time in custody?

Similarly, a proposed new Chief Executive for a new to-be-launched PLC was found to have withheld the fact that his previous company (he was chief executive) was involved with the Mafia in the USA and had been prosecuted for corruption and fined $26 million. A number of people had been murdered, machine gunned and had committed suicide.

The new legislation makes it clear that verification of customer(s) is very important and guidelines have been issued. For example, when verifying individuals, it is advised that the following checks should be considered:

- full name(s) used
- date and place of birth
- nationality
- current permanent address including post code
- telephone and fax number
- occupation and name of employer
- specimen signature
- documents including passport, national identity card, Armed Forces identity card and driving licence if it bears a photograph.

Most of these checks can be completed using credit databases, but it is important that such checks are not completed on face value. A recent investigation by a well known fraud investigator in London showed that he could obtain good credit references for Adolf Hitler, Lord Lucan and Napoleon Bonaparte.

We would like to open a bank account.

One has to ask the question whether the permanent home address as shown on an electoral roll is actually owned by the applicant or is the property rented. If owned, are the deeds in the applicant's or another name? In the UK, electoral rolls, land registry documents and such like can provide this important verification, but in other countries and jurisdictions such data is not so readily available.

We all know that a check of an employer or company may reveal an offshore organisation with nominee directors and we recommend that consideration should be given to:

- using a professional research agency should you not have the facilities to complete meaningful checks and/or

- apply a weighting system to the verification of the information supplied and set pass criteria.

Be suspicious of those customers who are reluctant to provide normal information or provide minimal, false or misleading information. Also the customer who provides information which is expensive for you to verify. You know the one – he has £2 million to invest and shows a Mongolian passport with an address 'Tent 6 – Umshal Ful U, Outer Mongolia'. These are obviously the ones that you need to report as suspicious.

However, proceed with caution. It may be worthwhile to check out the difficult information as the client may be genuine. One needs to make a commercial decision on whether it is worth spending money to verify the identity as the client may prove to be an excellent, genuine customer. It is matter of sifting out the genuine from the false.

It is also important that you are not driven by the promise of money where what looks like a good deal that will increase the bonus is pushed through the system without the appropriate caution being taken.

The legislation, as we shall detail later, affects banks, investment businesses, fiduciaries, the insurance market, money transmission services and so on.

All new account clients should be treated with caution and as verification subjects. This particularly applies to 'friends' introduced by current customers/clients – the old school tie is dead and offers little in mitigation if you are caught providing facilities to launder dirty money.

The importance of checking documents cannot be over-emphasised. With today's computer technology, forgeries are simple and the old control measures of signature verification are, to put it bluntly, useless. If in doubt, the services of a forensic expert can prove to be invaluable. Recently I contacted a company who were advertising various financial services such as offshore accounts, credit cards, work permits and other doubtful services such as anarchist handbooks. The proprietor advised that the Isle of Man was the best place to hide money as that is where he had hidden OJ Simpson's assets. This was probably no more than the proverbial bullshit, but what interested me was the offer of passports. He claimed that for £4,000 he could get me an African passport, and for £7,000 an Irish one. He advised that the more money I was prepared to spend, the better the jurisdiction of the passport. Obviously, the money launderer with all of his cash can afford to buy whatever he wishes. In other words, treat the production of a passport with caution. In fact the Portuguese Government has stated that many of their overseas consulates have been burgled with a large number of passports being stolen. As you will shortly read, Mr Kenneth Noye, one of the Brinks-Mat gold and money launderers, used false passports to conceal his identity.

Currently, it is estimated that there are about 20 million false identities in circulation in the United Kingdom, created by organised gangs who apply for new national insurance numbers and then create fictitious individuals who can then use the 'new number' to claim benefits and proof of identity for other frauds. The UK Government have admitted that there are 81 million NI numbers for a population of 60 million. Despite this problem, the government has scrapped the Data Cleaning Project which would have removed the bogus numbers in April 2001. As fraud is on the increase (false identity fraud has increased by 450% in 2001) this decision appears strange. Perhaps the 20 million are illegal immigrants, or it is a fiendish plot. Whatever the reason, and fraud is the obvious one, it highlights the need to pay more than lip-service to customer/client verification as it means that one in three NI numbers in circulation is false!

The following details what the regulatory bodies see as appropriate vigilance depending on what type of financial business you are operating. Obviously these recommendations are based on experience and should help prevent the money launderer using your business to launder their dirty money. I have analysed various guidelines and have divided the recommended vigilance deemed appropriate between the various types of financial businesses. So I apologise for the following boring bit, but it is essential reading for anyone with a responsibility for prevention of money laundering.

Banks & Financial Businesses

Banks should be vigilant when opening new accounts, doing business with non-account customers, accepting safe custody or safe deposit box business, deposit taking, lending and doing business involving marketing and self-promotion.
So what is suspicious?

Account Opening
As we mentioned a couple of pages back, take care with those customers who are reluctant to provide normal information or provides minimal, false or misleading information – the type who tells you that he works for an official agency and has been sworn to secrecy and if he tells you anything he may have to kill you.

Non-Account
All non-account clients should be treated with caution and as verification subjects. This particularly applies to 'friends' introduced by current customers/clients. It's no good thinking that all of your clients friends and associates are as honest and trustworthy as them.

Safe Deposit Boxes and safe custody facilities
Unless the customer is established and has been verified, extreme care should be taken in the acceptance of boxes, parcels and sealed envelopes. Full verification procedures should be taken especially in

respect of non-account customers. Our previous comments re non-account customers are relevant.

Deposit Taking

As explained, the criminal needs to get his dirty money into the banking system to initiate the cleaning cycle. The depositing of funds, usually cash, is often the only avenue open to him or her. So what deposits are suspicious? What do you look for? Unless you have a satisfactory explanation and can verify the source of the funds as being legitimate, substantial cash deposits, singly or in accumulations, should be regarded as suspicious. This is particularly relevant when the following factors apply.

- The business in which the customer is engaged would normally be conducted in cheques, bankers drafts, letters of credit, bills of exchange or other instruments, but not cash – especially such high amounts. In simple terms, large cash deposits from an international freight company would probably be suspicious.

- The cash deposit appears to be credited to the account for immediate conversion to a bankers order, money transfer or any other negotiable or readily marketable money instrument indicating rapid movements in and out of the account.

- Deposits are received by other banks and one becomes aware of the regular consolidation of such funds from those accounts prior to a request for onward wire transfer or transmission elsewhere. Only constant examination of the client's accounts would identify this trend.

- The customer or its representatives avoids direct contact with the bank.

- The use of nominee accounts, trustee accounts or client accounts appear to be unnecessary or inconsistent with the customer/ beneficiary's normal business.

- Numerous accounts are used when fewer would suffice for no apparent commercial reason (usually to disguise the scale of the deposits).

- Numerous individuals (especially people whose names do not appear on the account mandate) are used by the customer to make deposits.

- Frequent small deposits are made which, when taken together, are substantial.

- There is frequent switching of funds between accounts in different names and in different jurisdictions.

- Payments out of the account are made the same day and in the same amount as deposited that day.

- A substantial cash withdrawal is made from a previously dormant or inactive account.

- A substantial cash withdrawal is made from an account which has just received a large credit from overseas.

- Use is made of a third party (professional firm or trust company) to deposit cash or negotiable instruments, especially if these are immediately transferred between client or trust accounts.

- Use is made of bearer securities outside a recognised dealing system in settlement of an account or otherwise.

Lending

Very frequently, loans, mortgages and the issuing of credit and charge cards are used by money launderers at the layering or integration stages. Secured borrowing is an effective method of layering and integration because the legitimate financial business (the lender) has a genuine claim to the security of the loan between the criminal and those seeking to confiscate such assets.

Obviously if a law enforcement agency or prosecution service is granted, by a court, the seizure of a convicted criminal's assets (HM Customs & Excise usually seize any assets used in the completion of a crime – the American DEA have frequent auctions of aeroplanes, boats, exotic cars etc) and a financial business has a secure charge on that criminal's asset, expensive litigation may follow to ensure that the charge is honoured.

Marketing & Self Promotion

Should a customer not provide a satisfactory explanation to either:

- declining to provide information which would make them eligible for credit or other banking services, or

- makes insufficient use of normal banking facilities such as higher interest rates for large credit balances

they may be regarded as suspicious.

Electronic Transfers

In an effort to ensure that the SWIFT system is not used by money launderers, the Financial Task Force (FATF) have asked SWIFT to request that all users of the system when sending SWIFT MT100 messages (customer transfers) identify both remitting customer and recipient. Any customer who is reluctant to provide those details or provides details of a recipient who is located in an unregulated or loosely regulated jurisdiction and where criminal activity such as drug trafficking or terrorism is high, should be viewed as suspicious.

Investment Business

This type of business is not usually cash based and payments are made by cheque or transfer from another financial services business. The problem is that those payments can be from an unregulated bank by means of cheque, draft or wire transfer and there must be some responsibility to ensure that one knows who one is dealing with. Some experts will argue that such payments means that the Placement Stage has already been achieved and such transactions are in the Layering part of the wash cycle. Just because it has reached this stage, if all goes wrong and the wheel falls off, the fact that the crooks have laundered dirty money through your business is publicity that you will not want.

Obviously the payment of cash for investment products should be investigated fully as part of know-your-client.

As mentioned, the investment business is at risk at the layering stage as the liquidity of investment products is attractive to launderers as it allows them to quickly and easily move the criminal proceeds from one product to another, mixing them with lawful proceeds thus facilitating integration.

The risk of integration is also high as:

- opportunities to liquidate investment portfolios containing legal and illegal funds while concealing the latter are relatively easy

- the variety of available investments is extensive

- transfer between investment products is easy

Those investments at particular risk are:

- collective investment funds and other pooled funds (especially when unregulated)

- high risk/high reward products due to the fact that the launderer's cost of funds is by definition low and the potentially high rewards accelerate the integration and money laundering process.

Borrowing against security of investments

As mentioned previously, secured borrowing is an effective method of layering and integration because the legitimate financial business (the lender) has a genuine claim to the security of the loan made to the criminal and from those seeking to confiscate such assets.

Verification

Investment businesses will note the particular relevance in their case of exceptions to the need for verification, i.e.

Customers Dealing Direct

Where a customer deals with the investment business direct, the customer is the applicant for business to the investment business and accordingly determines who the verification subject(s) is(are). In exempt cases, as mentioned above, a record should be maintained indicating how the transaction arose and recording details of the paying financial services business branch sort code and account number or other financial services product reference number from which the cheque or payment is drawn.

Intermediaries and underlying customers

Where an agent/intermediary introduces a principal/customer to the investment business and the investment is made in the principal/customer's name, the principal/customer is the verification subject.

Nominees

Where an agent/intermediary acts for a customer (whether for a named client or through a client account) but deals in his own name, then the agent/intermediary is a verification subject (unless the applicant for business is an EC regulated financial services business) and the customer is also a verification subject.

If the applicant for business is an EC regulated or locally regulated financial services business, the fund manager may rely on an introduction from the applicant for business (or other written assurance that it will have verified any principal/customer for whom it acts as agent/intermediary). Such introductions should follow the verification procedures as detailed in know-your-customer procedures.

Delay in Verification

Where verification has not been completed in a reasonable time, then the business relationship or significant one-off transaction in question should not proceed any further.

Where an investor exercises cancellation rights, or cooling off rights, the repayment of money arising in these circumstances (subject to any shortfall deduction where applicable) does not constitute 'proceeding further with business'. As such cancellations can offer a route to launder money, investment businesses should be alert to any abnormal exercise of cancellation/cooling off rights by any investor, or in respect of business introduced through any single authorised intermediary. In the event that such an abnormal exercise of rights becomes apparent, the matter should be treated as suspicious and reported through the usual channels. In any case, repayment should not be made to a third party.

Redemption prior to completion of verification

If the transaction is a significant one-off transaction or is carried out within a business relationship, verification of the customer should be completed before the customer receives the proceeds of the redemption. Investment businesses can be considered to have taken reasonable measures of verification where payment is made:

- to the legal owner of the investment by means of cheque, where possible crossed 'account payee', or

- to a bank account held (solely or jointly) in the name of the legal owner of the investment by any electronic means of transferring funds.

Switch Transactions

There is no requirement for verification where it is a switch where all of the proceeds are directly reinvested in another investment which itself can, on subsequent resale, only result in either:

- a further reinvestment on behalf of the same customer
- a payment being made directly to him of which a record is kept.

Savings vehicles and regular investment programmes

Except in the case of a small one-off transaction, and subject to mandatory checks, where a customer has:

- agreed to make regular subscriptions or payments to an investment business
- arranged for the collection of such subscriptions or payments.

the investment business should undertake verification of the customer or satisfy themselves that such verification is exempt under the regulations.

Where the customer sets up a regular savings scheme where money invested by him is used to acquire investments to be registered in the name or held to the order of a third party, the person funding the cash transaction should be treated as the verification subject. When the investment is realised, the person who is then the legal owner (if not the person who funded it) should also to be treated as a verification subject.

Reinvestment of Income

A number of retail savings and investment vehicles offer customers the facility to have income reinvested. The use of such a facility is not seen as an entry into a business relationship and such reinvestments do not require verification of client.

Suspicious transactions

Unless one has a satisfactory explanation, the following transactions should be regarded as suspicious:

- introduction by an agent/intermediary in an unregulated or loosely regulated jurisdiction or a sensitive jurisdiction
- any delay or want in the provision of information thus hindering completion of verification
- any transaction involving an undisclosed party

- early termination especially at a loss caused by front end or rear end charges or early termination penalties
- transfer or assignment of the benefit of a product to an unrelated third party or assignment as collateral
- payment into the product by an unrelated third party
- use of bearer securities outside a recognised clearing system where a scheme accepts securities in lieu of payment.

Fiduciary Services

Many attorneys and financial businesses carry out fiduciary services in the setting up of trusts for clients. Unfortunately, with their inherent confidentiality, trust funds are a perfect place to launder dirty money.

It is considered good practice to ensure that key staff complete engagement documentation (client agreement etc) duly signed at the time of entry.

As with other financial service businesses, it is important that verification of new clients include:

- the verification of the settlor and/or the principal beneficiaries whenever a settlement is made or when accepting trusteeship from a previous trustee or where there are changes to principal beneficiaries or the settlor

- the verification of the identity of the underlying beneficial owners of any company that you have been requested to form

- documentation and information in respect of the new client for use by the administrator who has the daily management of the new client's affairs should include a note of any required further input on verification from any agent/intermediary of the new client, together with a deadline for the supply of such data.

Suspicious Transactions

In addition to the due diligence undertaken prior to and at the commencement of providing fiduciary services, there is an obligation to monitor the activities of the entities to which it provides services and in the absence of satisfactory explanation the following should be regarded as suspicious:

- any request for or the discovery of an unnecessarily complicated trust or corporate structure involving several different jurisdictions
- payments or settlements to or from an administered entity which are either of a size or source which had not been expected
- an administered entity entering into transactions which are either unrelated to the anticipated or have little or no obvious purpose
- use of bearer securities or cash outside a recognised clearing system in settlement of an account or otherwise
- the establishment of an administered entity with no obvious purpose
- sales invoice values that exceed the known or expected value of the goods/services
- sales or purchases at inflated or undervalued prices
- a large number of bank accounts or other financial products all receiving small payments which in total amount to a significant sum
- large payments of third party cheques endorsed in favour of the customer
- the use of nominees other than in the normal course of fiduciary business
- excessive use of wide-ranging powers of attorney
- unwillingness to disclose source of funds
- the use of PO boxes for no apparent advantage or necessity
- failure or tardiness to complete verification
- administered entities that constantly make substantial losses
- unnecessarily complex group structure
- unexplained subsidiaries
- high turnover of shareholders, directors, trustees or underlying beneficial owners

- the use of numerous different currencies for no apparent purpose
- arrangements established with the apparent objective of fiscal evasion.

Insurance

Offshore insurance business, whether life assurance, pensions or other risk management business, presents a number of opportunities to the criminal for money laundering at all of its stages. What can be easier than than paying cash for the purchase of a single premium product followed by early cancellation and reinvestment?

Examples of insurance products at risk from money launderers are:

- requests from clients to purchase insurance products where the source of funds to purchase the product is unclear or inconsistent with the customer's financial standing

- an urgent or sudden request for the purchase of a substantial policy with a lump sum payment by an existing client whose other policies etc are completely out of character with the new purchase

- any request for an insurance product that has no discernible purpose and a reluctance from the client(s) to divulge the reason for the investment

- to purchase an insurance product using a cheque drawn on a third party account

- client(s) who are not interested in the performance of the investment, but are more concerned about early cancellation and surrender value.

Verification requirements

Surrender prior to completion of verification

Whether the transaction is a significant one-off transaction or is carried out within a business relationship, verification of the client is required before they receive the surrender proceeds.

A life insurer is considered to have taken reasonable verification measures where payment is made either:

- to the policy holder by cheque crossed account payee, or
- to the bank account held in the name of the policyholder by electronic transfer.

Switch transactions

If the significant one-off transaction is switched to another policy of insurance where all of the proceeds are directly paid to the new policy and on surrender will result in:

- a further premium payment on behalf of the same client or
- a payment made directly to the client of which a record is kept

verification is not required.

Employer sponsored pension or savings schemes

In all transactions undertaken on behalf of an employer sponsored pension or savings scheme the insurer is required to undertake verification of:

- the principal employer; and
- the trustees of the scheme (if any)

and may need to verify the members if they as individuals seek personal investment advice unless the employer/trustees have been verified and the principal employer confirms the identity and address of the investor in writing.

Suspicious Transactions

- applications from potential clients from overseas for business where a comparable service can be provided closer to home
- application for business outside the insurer's normal pattern of business
- any introduction from an agent/intermediary in either an unregulated or loosely regulated jurisdiction or where criminal activity is prevalent
- any delay in the provision of information needed for verification purposes or the lack of the full details required
- any proposal involving an undisclosed third party
- early termination of product especially at a loss caused by front end loading, or where cash was tendered and/or the refund cheque is to a third party
- 'churning' at the client's request
- transfer of the product's benefit to an unrelated third party
- use of bearer securities outside the recognised clearing system in settlement of an account
- insurance premiums higher than market levels
- large, unusual or unverifiable insurance claims
- unverified reinsurance premiums
- large introductory commissions
- insurance policies for unusual/unlikely exposures

Summary

The Joint Money Laundering Steering Group, the Jersey/Guernsey Financial Services Commissions and Isle of Man Supervision Commission have given general guidance on verification. The main points made are as follows.

- A financial services business undertaking verification should establish that every verification subject relevant to the application for business actually exists.

• All of the joint applicants for business should be verified

• Where there are a large number of verification subjects, it may be sufficient to carry out full verification on a limited group such as senior members of a family, principal shareholders, main directors etc

• Primarily, the verification should be in respect of the parties operating the financial services product. Where there are underlying principals, the true nature of the relationship between the principals and signatories should be established and verification completed on these principals especially where the signatories act on the instructions of the principals. These principals will include beneficial owners, settlors, controlling shareholders, directors, major beneficiaries etc. The level of verification will depend on the exact nature of the relationship.

Know your clients and employees

2

The Classic Cases

The Lansky Legacy

It's better in the Bahamas

*'You can buy an airstrip, or an island. You can buy citizenship.
You can buy protection. You can buy justice. And should your
drug cargo get seized by the Police, you can even buy it back.'*
Carl Hiaasen and Jim McGee
'A Nation for Sale', *Miami Herald*, 23 September 1984

Meyer Lansky was one of the first criminals to use his brain rather
than muscle. Born in Poland and raised in New York, a 9th grade drop
out, he became the highest ranking non-Italian in what was called The
Syndicate, and was known as the mob's accountant. Today he is
remembered as the patron saint of money launderers.

When Al Capone was sent to prison for tax evasion, Lansky had a
theory:

*'Any money that the Inland Revenue Service does not know
about is not taxable.'*

He then embarked on a search of ways to hide money and he quickly
discovered the benefits of numbered Swiss bank accounts. Later he
became instrumental in financing The Flamingo as a casino/hotel

complex in a small Nevada town that was to grow into the gambling capital of the world, Las Vegas. What better way to launder the proceeds of crime.

He then convinced the mob to take their 'income' offshore, first to Havana with the blessing of President Batista, and then with the arrival of Castro, who threw the Americans out, to the Bahamas. Money from the United States was laundered through the Casino in Nassau where it became Casino profit deposited into local banks and then transferred back to various accounts in the USA.

Lansky secured the Bahamas as the mob's offshore financial centre by funding Lynden Pindling, a self styled 'Black Moses of the people', in his political aspirations. Pindling became Prime Minister and a corrupt regime ensued. Only this year, have the Bahamas Government addressed the problem of money laundering with new legislation being enacted to clean up the island's image and to become accepted by FATF as being a cooperative financial jurisdiction. Their legislation calls for the reporting of 'unusual' transactions as opposed to 'suspicious'.

In the 1970s, the Bahamas began to woo Colombian and other drug traffickers and the islands were used as airfields and harbours for drugs in transit to nearby Florida and the Carolinas.

A Royal Commission formed in the 1980s to investigate the drug trade in the Bahamas found corruption in the courts, police and government. Pindling and other ministers were found to have deposited millions of pounds in excess of their salaries into various bank accounts.

Local banking laws with strict secrecy regulations, which make local banking officials from manager to teller criminally liable if they reveal details about their clients and their transactions, made it impossible for foreign law enforcement agents to investigate suspect transactions.

Money arrived originally stuffed in beer cartons (Meyer) and later in suitcases, bin liners and so on. Bank tellers were paid a commission to count the money, this being usually 2%. After safely depositing the cash, it was wire transferred to a foreign bank. North Americans preferred Canadian or US banks, whereas Colombians preferred

Panamanian banks. To conceal the money trail even more, Bahama shell companies with nominee directors were set up and funds were paid into bank accounts in the shell company name from where it was wire transferred to another shell company in Panama.

To show the growth of the Bahamas drug trade, one only has to look at The Royal Bank of Canada's Bimini branch who, in 1977, transferred only $0.5 million to the Nassau branch, yet by 1984 that figure had increased to over $24 million. These transactions were all in respect of cash deposits. The bank, when asked, could not identify the funds coming from any ordinary business transaction. Bimini has a local population of 2,000, and 500 allegedly work in the drug trade.

The Bahamas banking system was dominated by Canadian banks. Of the six most important banks, four were Canadian and the other two were British and American. When American and Canadian authorities became frustrated with the Canadian banks' lax attitude to money laundering, they were stonewalled by the banks who claimed that the Bahamas banks operated under Bahamas law, not Canadian. However the US investigators eventually won a landmark court decision and the Bank of Novia Scotia was fined $1.8 million.

Subsequently, the other banks set up anti-money laundering procedures, but there was no noticeable decline in dollar deposits. Bimini has been shut down as a drug centre and the Royal Navy and American agencies have reduced the volume of actual drug traffic through the islands. Stopping the traffic does not of course stop the money laundering. However, as mentioned, new legislation currently being enacted has improved the anti-money laundering controls and regulations in this jurisdiction. Notwithstanding, Lansky certainly left a legacy of awesome proportions.

Tricky Dicky

It was in 1973 that the term money laundering first appeared in print and it was reported as such during the Watergate scandal. In 1972, Richard Nixon took the first steps to secure his tenure of the White House and created a committee – The Committee to Re-elect the

President – ' CRP' bizarrely pronounced 'creep' although in retrospect, I can think of better pronunciation.

Nixon's formal law partner, Attorney General John Mitchell, was named to run CRP, but the real drive began a year earlier when Mitchell, and Secretary Maurice Stans, began building a war chest. Major donors were the American Dairy Industry (Nixon had raised milk subsidies) and Howard Hughes who is reported to have handed $100,000 to Nixon's closest friend, Florida banker, Charles 'Bebe' Rebozo. Disgraced financier Robert Vesco, who at the time was under investigation by the Justice Department, arranged a cash donation of $200,000.

Mitchell and Stans approached American Airlines for $100,000 and the chairman, George Spater, was faced with the predicament of how to divert corporate funds that were otherwise accountable. He contacted a Lebanese company called Amarco and asked them to submit a false invoice for commission on sales of aircraft parts to Middle East Airlines. The $100,000 was paid and Amarco deposited the funds into their Swiss bank account from where it was wire transferred to their account in New York. Their New York agent withdrew the money in cash and paid it to Spater who passed it on to Mitchell and Stans.

Braniff Airlines, who needed to raise and hide a $40,000 donation, similarly arranged for a false invoice to be submitted to their Panama office for goods and services. They then supplied the office with a batch of unaccountable blank tickets which were sold to passengers who paid cash for their airline tickets. This money was funnelled through a Dallas construction company before showing up in Braniff's books to cover the shortfall.

Ashland Oil arranged a similar scheme, the money coming from their Gabob subsidiary and washed through Switzerland from where it was withdrawn in cash and carried back to the USA in an executive briefcase. Gulf Oil laundered their donation through their subsidiary in the Bahamas.

As congress were about to pass legislation about the reporting of donations and prohibiting anonymous ones, Mitchell and Stans decided to raise as much as possible before the deadline. Using an old

Mexican connection that would guarantee such donations could not be traced, they targeted private citizens as well as other corporations.

Among the donations, were four cashiers' cheques totalling $89,000, all made out by different American banks, and payable to a Mexico City lawyer, Manuel Ogarrio Daguerre. The four cheques were mailed to Miami where they were paid into a bank account of a real estate salesman, Bernard L Barker. He was instructed that, if questioned about the funds, to say that it was his share of a land deal with an anonymous Chilean businessman. If then asked why he withdrew the $89,000 in cash, he was to answer that the deal fell through and he had to repay the commission.

Then it all went wrong. Our intrepid pair decided to use some of the fund to finance a burglary at Watergate. Even after the quick arrest of the five burglars, our duo did not think that anyone would be able to discover and trace funds paid to CRP. However, after the Washington Post scoop, every journalist in the USA wanted to get in on the act.

The New York Times discovered the Mexican connection and investigators got into Barker's bank account and found a fifth cheque payable to a Nixon Fund raiser in the Mid West. When interviewed, he admitted that he had paid it to Stans. Further investigations revealed that CRP had washed $750,000 through Mexico and that Stans had a huge cash slush fund in his office at CRP.

The irony of this case was that, in 1973, money laundering was not illegal anywhere in the world.

The treasure of La Mina

La Mina is Spanish for The Mine and Colombia's drug cartels dubbed one of their money laundering organisations with that name.

In 1991, Vahe and Nazareth Andonian, together with Raoul Vivas, were sentenced to 505 years imprisonment without parole. They had laundered drug monies for the Colombian Medellin cartel and the proceeds of heroin sales from Turkish drug traffickers.

The Andonians were in the jewellery business in Los Angeles and when La Mina was discovered, it had been operating for some 15 years. Due to pressure from the law enforcement agencies in Florida, the Colombians had relocated to Los Angeles. By the late 1980s, LA banks were producing a $3.8 billion cash surplus – a 2,200% increase in four years.

Basically the banks were awash with cash deposits and, as they had more cash than needed for normal daily business, the surplus was paid into the Federal Reserve Bank. Whereas in the rest of the USA, the Federal Reserve Bank was reporting a deficit of some $16.5 billion, Southern California was in surplus.

Vivas was approached by the Colombian drug cartels with an offer that he could not refuse. On the table was the offer of a 5% handling fee to launder $500 million a year. He immediately formed two front companies in Montevideo, Letra SA to deal in gold, and Cambio Italia SA to operate as a currency exchange business. An office was opened in the Los Angeles jewellery centre at 610 South Broadway in the heart of the city's diamond trading district.

The plan was simple – all of the drug money collected around the USA would be sent to a front company in New York's jewellery district from where it would be taken by courier to the Los Angeles office. Vivas used this money to purchase gold in all of its various forms where the dealer was prepared to accept cash payment at a purchase price over the odds. The gold materials would be melted down and mixed with silver so that it represented South American gold.

Dummy gold was then exported to the USA by Letra with appropriate documentation, the dummy gold was destroyed on receipt and replaced with the newly smelted 'South American' gold. This gold was sold in New York and the now laundered, clean, money from the sales wired to Cambio Italiana who paid Letra SA who in turn paid the money to the Colombians.

Due to the large amounts of cash being handled by Vivas, the system was in danger of collapse so he brought the Andonian brothers, who operated a number of jewellery businesses, and a Syrian, Wanis Koyomejian, who operated a gold dealing company Ropex, into the scheme.

As the business expanded even further, Vivas brought in friends in Miami, Houston and New York.

Meanwhile the Medellin cartel's financial representative Eduardo Martinez Romero was introduced to a New York mafia-connected drug trafficker, Jimmy Brown, and during their first meeting he bragged about the Vivas' 'La Mina' operation. Brown suggested a separate laundering operation through Atlanta and some $12 million was laundered through that city.

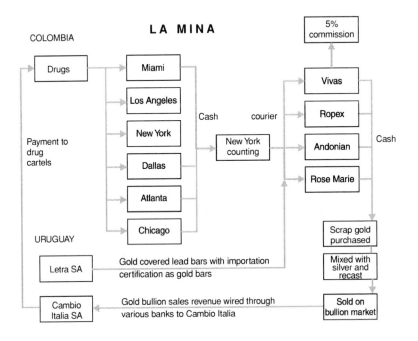

However, $1 million of drugs money was seized by the authorities in Atlanta and at a meeting between Romero, Brown, and an associate Alex Carrera, in Panama, Romero insisted that the $1 million be paid back by Brown. At a second meeting in Aruba between the same parties, plus the man in charge of the Atlanta operation, Romero, after too many drinks, boasted again about La Mina, claiming that it had washed $28 million in the last 45 days with a wash cycle of 48 hours. It was agreed that the Atlanta operation would take a commission cut to 6% to repay the lost $1 million and match the 48 hour wash cycle. Romero continued to brag over the next few months, being unaware that Brown's real name was John Featherly, and Carrera's real name was Cesar Diaz (both being undercover Drug Enforcement Agency agents) and that the Atlanta operation was being run by the Agency as a sting.

In San Francisco, a bank officer at Wells Fargo Banking Corporation, noted that the Andonian brothers had, in just under three months, deposited $25 million in cash into an account at one of the branches. He telephoned the Internal Revenue Service.

At Los Angeles Airport, a shipping clerk was checking a cargo of scrap gold from a jeweller in New York being sent to a gold dealer called Ropex in Los Angeles. One of the boxes was ripped open and he noted that it contained, not gold, but cash. He reported it to his management who contacted Ropex. Ropex claimed that there had been a mix up and that they knew all about it. The cash was from the jeweller hoping to find better short term interest rates in Los Angeles. The shipping company sent the cargo to Ropex, but being unhappy with Ropex's explanation, notified the FBI.

A surveillance operation code named 'Polar Cap' was initiated with hidden video cameras throughout the Los Angeles jewellery district and in New York. Phone taps were placed on various telephones, people were followed and garbage was collected. The garbage included various documents such as invoices with contacts in Canada, Mexico, and the United Kingdom, plus cancelled cheques identifying bank accounts as well as lists of friendly gold dealers. The operation became the biggest in the history of US law enforcement.

A task force from the FBI, Drug Enforcement Agency, Internal Revenue Service, Customs and Bureau of Alcohol, Tobacco and Firearms, plus the US Immigration and Naturalisation Service arrested everyone. Evidence of 1035 bank accounts in 179 banks throughout the Americas and Europe was found. 127 indictments were served and Vivas and Romero were extradited to the USA. Some $1.2 billion had been laundered. The US authorities not only seized assets and froze bank accounts, but fined foreign banks with US branches for their wilful participation in La Mina.

The investigation spread to Switzerland where the first female Justice Minister, Elizabeth Kopp, resigned in the wake of her husband's involvement in money laundering where it was found that his company Shakarchi Trading was involved with drugs money seized in Los Angeles, it being en route to his company from the Andonian brothers. He also had meetings in Zurich with representatives from Ropex.

Elements of this case and the recent expose of Liechtenstein's dubious activities highlight the use of technology to identify money launderers' activities. In the United Kingdom, GCHQ at Cheltenham and the US Secret Service communication centre in Yorkshire, monitor communications, whether telephone, satellite, internet or whatever, between locations where national security may be threatened. Obviously the activities of organised crime are subject to surveillance. Recently the national press revealed that e-mails are to be subject of surveillance.

In effect, this means that, should your business become involved in money laundering, it is likely that communications from your business will be monitored. With the ever-increasing use of cctv systems in town centres for security purposes, evidence of a target money launderer entering your premises is readily available.

The seizure of garbage in this case and the discovery of evidence is worthy of comment. During an investigation into money laundering in London, garbage dumped on the pavement outside a private bank in Mayfair was examined by me, and although it did not identify any evidence of money laundering, highly confidential personal bank account data was discovered. I had the account details and bank balances of most of Hollywood's movie star population. This data could of course be used by the criminal fraternity.

As one can see from the flowchart opposite, the money laundering in this case was quite a simple scheme that collapsed due to errors being made by the main players involved. The drugs cash was placed in the system by using it to purchase gold and silver for cash, the gold/silver was then resmelted and layered into the genuine gold market by using it to replace 'false' gold imports, and the resulting clean funds from the sale of that 'South American' gold were integrated back to the drug cartels.

Brinks-Mat

I have include this case as it contains all of the elements of classic money laundering with some similarities to La Mina.

On 26 November 1983, several criminals broke into the Brinks-Mat warehouse near London's Heathrow airport. After terrorising the guards they entered the underground vaults and stole 6,400 gold bars with a market value of £ 26,369, 778.

Within a month, the police had four of the men in custody and a year later three of the four were sentenced to 25 years imprisonment. Unfortunately, the police had still not recovered one ounce of the stolen gold.

One of the three convicted men, Mickey McAvoy had friends including the owner of a mini-cab firm, Brian Perry, and John Lloyd who lived with Jeannie Savage (her husband was serving 22 years for armed robbery). Perry and Lloyd contacted Kenneth Noye to help them dispose of the gold. Unlike Perry or Lloyd, Noye had a criminal record and at the time of the robbery was the subject of an investigation by HM Customs & Excise officers looking into gold smuggling and a tax fraud scheme. Using his obvious experience, Noye contacted a John Palmer who had a gold bullion dealership in Bristol called Scadlynn Limited. Also involved in Scadlynn was Garth Chappell who had previously been convicted of conspiracy to defraud.

Noye decided that the gold could be laundered through Scadlynn but it was essential that the serial numbers on each bar were removed. Palmer, who owned his own smelter agreed to melt the gold down and then recast it prior to shipping to Scadlynn. The plan was then to melt the gold again, but mix it with copper and silver coins so that it looked like scrap bullion. This would then be taken to the government Assay Office in Sheffield where each bar would be weighed, taxed and legitimised. Scadlynn would be then free to sell it to licensed bullion dealers who as middlemen would melt the impurities out and market it to the British jewellery trade.

Noye knew from experience that he had to protect himself and flew to Jersey in 1984 where he took £50,000 in £50 notes to Charterhouse Japhet Bank, Bath St, St.Helier. Officials at the bank

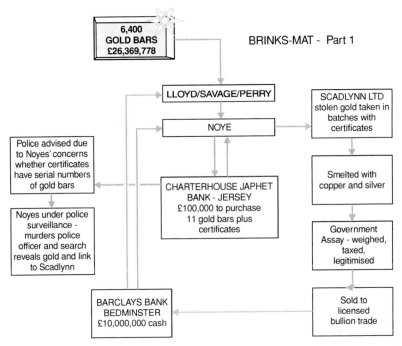

agreed to purchase 11 one-kilo gold bars. At this stage Noye made his first mistake – he kept asking the officials for their assurance that the certificates issued with each bar did not show the bars' serial number. Despite their assurances, he kept asking the question, claiming that if the certificates did show the serial numbers, the deal was off. Finally he accepted their assurances and left the £50,000 as the deposit and returned to London.

The balance of £50,000 was sent to the bank and 8 days later, Noye flew back to Jersey and collected the gold bars and certificates.

He deposited the gold bars in a safe deposit box at the New Street branch of the TSB and flew home with the certificates. It was no accident that he purchased 11 bars and that they matched the stolen gold in size and content. 11 bars weigh 11 kilos or just over 24 pounds and can be carried easily in a briefcase with a nice round value of £100,000. The mistake he had made was that his concerns about the certificates had aroused the suspicions of the bank officials who informed the local police. During his second visit, he was followed and before he landed back in England, the police in the UK had been alerted.

Placement – the gold was now in the system

He could now take 11 bars at a time to Scadlynn and, if stopped, had the certificates as an insurance policy. The arrangement was that Scadlynn would charge the going scrap rate plus VAT. Scadlynn was allowed to keep the undeclared VAT as their profit.

The money would be deposited in the local Barclays Bank at Bedminster in Bristol, where it was withdrawn in cash and paid to Noye, Perry and Lloyd. In five months some £10 million was sent to the three men, usually in black plastic bags in the boot of a car or lorry.

Using a false passport in the name Sydney Harris, Noye deposited his share of the cash into an account with the Bank of Ireland at Croydon. A standing arrangement meant that it was immediately wire transferred to the bank's Dublin office. McAvoy's girlfriend Kathy Meacock and Jeannie Savage used the same Croydon branch on alternative days to make deposits also wired to Dublin.

Meanwhile, Perry had brought in Gordon Parry and a solicitor, Michael Relton. Parry, with Relton's help, deposited £793,500 in cash from Scadlynn into the Bank of Ireland's Balham branch where it was instantly wired to the bank's Douglas, Isle of Man branch. Parry's wife's cousin also helped and deposited a further £500,000 at Balham where it was wired to the Isle of Man.

To confuse anyone attempting to follow the money trail, Parry brought some of the money in the Isle of Man back to the Balham branch into a second account from where it was withdrawn in dribs and drabs to be sent offshore to another bank. During all of this time, the stolen gold was still being sent to Scadlynn for processing.

In August 1984, using a solicitor's introduction from Relton, Parry opened an account at the Hong Kong & Shanghai Bank in Zurich, where he deposited £840,435 in cash. A week later, an unidentified man walked in‡to the bank's Bishopsgate headquarters in London with a sports bag containing £500,000 in cash. He instructed the bank to send it to Zurich.

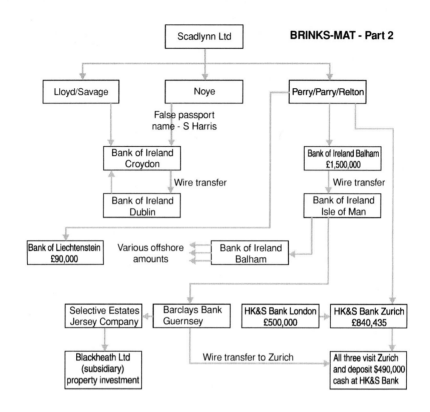

Layering – the cash proceeds were now being circulated to confuse and hide

A few weeks later, Perry, Parry, Relton, a jeweller named Elcombe with his wife, all met in Zurich and opened accounts at the same branch of the HK & S bank. Another £490,000 cash was deposited. Perry and Parry nipped across the border into Liechtenstein where they both opened an account at the Bank of Liechtenstein with £45,000 cash.

Parry then purchased an off-the-shelf company in Jersey called Selective Estates. An account for the company was opened at Barclays Bank in Guernsey and money from the Isle of Man was transferred into that account. Selective Estates wired those funds from

Guernsey to a second HK & S account in Zurich.

In September, Elcombe deposited £65,000 in cash into his Zurich account and the same day Parry walked into the Bank of Liechtenstein with a suitcase containing £500,000 in cash. A few weeks later, Elcombe paid £1,075,000 cash into his Zurich account. So much money was going through Barclays at Bedminster that extra staff were transferred in to cope with the cash.

Noye's Jersey mistake now took a serious turn as the Police, who had been keeping an eye on him after being alerted by the Jersey police, had spotted him meeting with a wanted criminal, Brian Reader. C11, the Metropolitan Police specialist intelligence gathering team, were called in and in January 1985, they placed Noye's house under surveillance. Noye discovered one of the officers in his garden and the officer was murdered. Noye and Reader were arrested and charged with murder. Ten months later, a jury acquitted them both, but there was enough evidence found at Noye's house to link them with the Brinks-Mat robbery, a small cache of gold bars being found.

Within three days, Palmer and Chappell at Scadlynn had been arrested and that company's affairs were being investigated. On the day the officer was murdered, Elcombe and his wife had left London in Parry's Mercedes with £710,000 in cash stowed in the boot. Two weeks previously, they had made a cash deposit of £453,000 in cash to their account in Zurich.

On the way to Zurich, they were stopped at Aachen by border guards. When asked if they had any money, they declared £45,000, which was their life savings, which they were taking to Switzerland. The guard decided to search the car and found the £710,000 cash under the carpet in the boot. The Elcombes now changed their story and claimed to be antique dealers working out of Belgium. They were detained for questioning. The money was taken out of the car and counted in the border guards' hut where, for some reason, he made a note of serial numbers on a random basis. The German Interpol office was advised and they contacted the British Interpol office. As nothing was recorded about Elcombe, nor whether large amounts of currency had been stolen or the car reported stolen, the Elcombes were released with the cash. However, an officer at Scotland Yard saw the telex messages and that the car was registered to Parry. The name rang a bell and then he realised Parry was linked to the Brinks-Mat investigation, A phone call to the Brinks-Mat situation room confirmed his suspicions and when the team there heard the name Elcombe they begged Interpol to stop them – but it was too late, they had long gone.

On arrival in Zurich, Elcombe deposited £100,000 in his account and opened a new account (720.3) in which he deposited £608,000. A few days later, someone deposited £493,970 in Parry's Liechtenstein account and a week after the murder, Elcombe transferred £1.6 million from his initial account at HK&S Zurich to the new 720.3 account. Parry then closed his Liechtenstein account and transferred the funds to the 720.3 account.

Relton, the solicitor, went to Liechtenstein in April and opened a 'Red Cross account'. These are used by attorneys and tax specialists as foundation accounts, the funds being controlled by an organisation often in the name of a charity under the administration of an attorney. In effect, this type of account usually has written into its charter that a charity is the named beneficiary, the beneficiary is not necessarily the beneficial owner of the account. No one is supposed to know who that is, not even the bank's directors. The true identity is protected by a double layer of bank secrecy and attorney-client privilege. Robert Maxwell used such accounts in Liechtenstein and duly claimed that neither he or his family controlled the funds he deposited there or would benefit from them.

Relton opened this account in the name Moet Foundation, spelt by the bank Moyet. (Moet was Relton's favourite champagne). Relton and Parry deposited £3,167,409.25 into this account. Parry at this stage also made a vital mistake when he paid for a farm purchase with a draft drawn on the 720.3 account in the amount £152,126. He had not checked whether there were funds in the account to cover the draft and in the haste to transfer funds to the new Moyet account, they had not checked to see whether the draft had cleared. Because the bank knew where the funds had gone, they simply transferred the funds back from Moyet to cover the draft. This enabled the Police to identify the Moyet account and its links to the robbers.

Some 15 months had elapsed since the robbery and there was probably only £5 million of gold left. Relton and Parry decided to invest for the future and embarked on a series of property investments. Using the Jersey registered company Selective Estates as an umbrella, they set up a subsidiary called Blackheath Limited. To finance a property purchase in Cheltenham, they wove a complex web of transactions:

1. Relton transferred $300,000 from HK&S Bank Zurich to South East Bank Sarasota, Florida where he had an account.

2. From there, he sent $200,000 to his personal account at Midland Bank, London.

3. He then sent £104,000 to The British Bank of the Middle East (a London subsidiary of HK&S).

4. They wired £103,700 to the solicitors acting for the sellers of the Cheltenham property.

5   Relton then borrowed £250,000 from the British Bank of the Middle East using his account at HK&S Zurich as security.

The pair used the same money moving scheme again, this time including Jersey, Guernsey and the Isle of Man in the washing cycle. Some £2.1 million was laundered this way and the pair descended on London's Docklands, purchasing several wharfs for £5.4 million and using what looked like legitimate loans to conceal the true origin of the money.

Integration had been achieved

With Noyes' arrest and discovery of the gold at his house, the police investigation into the missing gold and proceeds of the subsequent sale by the criminals led to the arrest of various gang members. All except the Elcombes became guests of Her Majesty and, remember

Mr McAvoy? You know, the one who stole the gold in the first place. All he ended up with was a lengthy prison sentence and when released, I suspect he will be looking for a few people who lost him his ill-gotten fortune. In fact, teams of detectives recently descended on a site in Kent associated with McAvoy and proceeded to search for gold allegedly buried there.

With hindsight, it is easy to see where proper anti-money laundering controls may have hindered the criminals. Only one financial institution contacted the authorities and that was not because Noye turned up with £50,000 in cash, but because he kept asking about the serial numbers on the certificates that came with the gold he purchased.

Noye, since his release from prison, continued his life of crime, using false passports to escape to Spain after the M25 road rage murder and allegedly buying a Spanish villa for cash, plus other real estate. One wonders how effective Spanish money laundering laws are?

If anyone is interested, the 11 bars, worth at that time £100,000, remain in a Boots carrier bag within the safe deposit box at TSB in St.Helier. The box number and password to obtain the gold is .... Actually, there was quite a peculiar twist to this story. When Noye was recently convicted of murder at The Old Bailey, the press made enquiries in Jersey to confirm the whereabouts of this gold. It seems to have disappeared.

Recently, the press reported that Marbella on the good old Costa del Crime has become a paradise for money launderers and drug dealers. No wonder Noye decamped to Spain to be with his old associates. Palmer, the Scadlynn smelter, has recently been involved in an alleged massive time share scam in the Canaries, and the trial at the Old Bailey has ended as a mis-trial. Until the details of that case become public, one can but speculate as to where the money came from to build all of these apartments in the Canaries.

The laughing policeman

One of the richest policeman that you will usually see is the one in the glass case at the end of the pier. You know the one, little children are constantly feeding him money through a slot to make him laugh.

On a more serious note, Anthony Williams, ex-Deputy Director of Finance, New Scotland Yard, made much more. Using his position of trust, he stole some £8 million from his employers over an 8 year period and was finally caught when someone became suspicious of the source of his wealth.

In 1984, Williams was entrusted with the purchase of an aircraft to be used for secret surveillance operations. It was decided to form a private company as cover so Turnbull Associates was formed, with a West London accommodation address. The company purchased a Cessna 404 and based it at Fairoaks airfield. Williams was entrusted with signing cheques in the name D G Turnbull to finance the operation.

On Day One, he stole £3,400 to clear his bank overdraft. Waiting two weeks to see whether the theft was noted, he started to increase the amounts stolen, purchasing a mansion in the country, a flat in London, a villa in Spain, and various properties in and around the village of Tomintoul, Scotland, plus a few cars and expensive holidays.

Although the Yard had implemented audits and simple security measures to detect such anomalies, Williams had been requested to keep the aircraft operation secret and it was he that recommended the setting up of Turnbull Associates with sole control being in his hands. When a superior disagreed and sent a written memo outlining his objections, Williams doctored the memo so that it supported his own ideas.

Once a month, Williams drew up a requisition for funds for the Turnbull account which was primarily fuel and rent, but Williams added a few bogus items for himself. Once he received the money, he wrote cheques to himself and, as time elapsed without discovery, stopped forging invoices and just demanded more money. When threatened with an audit he used the 'need to know' doctrine to stop the auditors and even requested that they make a sworn oath of secrecy (which was not forthcoming) and the threat of audit disappeared.

He then purchased a title and became Lord Williams, formed a company, Tomintoul Enterprises Limited to develop the village and build a hotel.

He then (as with most criminals) made his mistake, requesting a development grant from Moray, Grathspey and Baldenoch Enterprise Board to construct the hotel. Mr Ruane of the Board was prepared to grant £150,000 to refurbish the hotel but requested that Tomintoul Enterprises reveal the source of their funds. Mr Ruane could not understand how someone with a salary of £42,000 could invest millions of pounds into the venture.

When William's bank did not answer requests for details of his funds, the matter was reported to the National Criminal Intelligence Service. Williams was arrested shortly after.

I helped launder £6 billion for the mob

The latest, and some say the biggest, money laundering case of all, has recently hit the news headlines. I have included this case as the evidence so far presented poses important questions.

Peter Berlin and his wife Lucy Edwards, a London-based Bank of New York official, Benex International Company Inc ('Benex'), Becs International L.L.C. ('Becs'), and Lowland Inc ('Lowland') appeared at Manhattan Federal Court on 16 February 2000 where all pleaded guilty to various charges including conspiracy to commit money laundering, operating an unlawful banking and money transmitting business, plus aiding and abetting Russian banks in conducting unlawful, unlicenced banking activities in the United States.

They admitted that between late 1995 and September 1999 they participated with others in establishing an illegal banking network that transmitted more than $7 billion through accounts held in the Bank of New York. Specifically they admitted that they:

- conducted unlicenced and unregulated banking operations
- established an unauthorised branch of a foreign bank
- operated an illegal money transmitting business
- laundered money through international fund transfers intending to promote criminal activity including a scheme to defraud the Russian Government of customs duties and tax revenues

- made corrupt payments to a bank employee
- received corrupt payments as a bank officer
- laundered these corrupt payments abroad
- evaded the payment of individual income taxes to the US
- fraudulently obtained visas for Russian nationals to enter the USA

In addition Berlin and Edwards also pleaded guilty to assisting two banks, Depozitarno Kliringovy Bank ('DKB') and Commercial Bank Flamingo ('Flamingo') in establishing branches and agencies in the USA which then conducted illegal, unauthorised banking activities. Benex, Becs and Lowland also admitted conducting an illegal money transmitting service.

The story all started in late 1995 when Berlin and Edwards entered an agreement with various, to date unnamed, individuals, including those that controlled DKB, to open an account in Bank of New York to gain access to banking software – Micro/cash-register – which would enable wire transfers to be made in the new account by themselves. In early 1996, Berlin opened a corporate account in the name BENEX, who were authorised by the Bank of New York to use the software, which was installed in a computer in the offices of General Forex, Forest Hills, Queens, New York.

General Forex was managed on behalf of DKB and the company later changed its name to Torfinex. Using several Russian correspondents' accounts held at Bank of New York, DKB transferred funds into the Benex account on a daily basis. DKB then issued instructions, from its Moscow base, to Torfinex employees in Queens to transfer funds out of the BENEX account using the software to a large number of third party accounts throughout the world. British Intelligence allege that some of these funds were paid to drug barons, contract killers and to YBM Magex. (more about YBM and its money laundering operation is included later).

In July 1996, a second account was opened called BECS, again the Bank of New York provided software and the same cash movements ensued.

In the Autumn of 1998, Berlin and Edwards were allegedly told that the Flamingo Bank in Russia was being taken over by the Russians behind the original scheme and a new account was opened by Berlin called Lowland. The computer software was issued and set up in an office rented by the Russians in Jersey City, New Jersey. In April 1999, funds were directed into the Lowland account and then wire transferred out to various third parties all over the world.

BANK OF NEW YORK

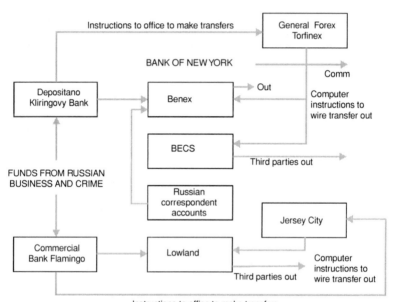

Instructions to office to make transfers

Berlin and Edwards moved to London where she became senior official in charge of the bank's East European operations. She even presented a paper on money laundering at a European Banking Conference. To keep control of the three accounts, they recruited another bank employee, Sventla Kudryavtsev, to manage the accounts and act as a contact with the Torfinex staff. This employee was paid $500 a month by the two for this 'service' and details of all wire transfers through the three accounts were sent to London so that Berlin and Edwards could calculate their commissions.

The Republic Bank in the USA filed a suspicious activity report in August 1998 and the FBI commenced an investigation that involved a number of law enforcement agencies including NCIS in London.

It is important to note that no commercial activity took place by these three companies and the accounts were used to facilitate:

- the transfer of funds out of Russia in violation of currency control limitations and to promote schemes to defraud he Russian Government of duties and taxes

- other criminal activities including the payment of $300,000 in ransom to the kidnappers of a Russian businessman in Russia

The investigation has initially revealed that some $7 billion went through the three accounts at Bank of New York. This equated to hundreds of wire transfers a day in respect of BENEX and BECS accounts, and dozens a day in respect of the LOWLAND account. From February 1996 until August 1999, there were some 160,000 wire transfers. Benex has also been linked with one of the major Russian mafia 'dons' Mogilevitch (see the next case – The Russians).

Berlin and Edwards received some $1.8 million in commissions which they hid by laundering in foreign bank accounts. To date they have forfeited $1 million in proceeds which include the contents of 2 Swiss bank accounts, a securities brokerage account and their London residence. The three companies have agreed to forfeiture of some $6 million held in the accounts at Bank of New York.

The investigation continues with the Swiss authorities now requesting to question the Russian Prime Minister, Mikhail Kasyanov, about a $4.8 billion International Monetary Fund loan which, it is alleged, he laundered through foreign bank accounts after the August 1998 financial crash in Russia. It is alleged that he was involved in a series of complex transfers by which the loan never reached Russia but was absorbed into commercial accounts in the West.

The investigation by the Swiss and FBI has linked the 'missing' funds to the Bank of New York case and unproven allegations of inside knowledge prior to the financial crash has resulted in his nickname of 'Misha Two Per Cent'. Most of the loan has ended up in American accounts belonging to 18 commercial Russian Banks of which many have ceased trading. Investigators have established that on August 14, 1998, some $4.8 billion was transferred from the New York Federal Reserve to accounts at the Republic Bank of New York (the bank that blew the whistle on the Bank of New York). This bank was controlled by Edmund Safra, the billionaire Lebanese banker. He was killed in a fire at his Monte Carlo residence last year and although the death has been blamed on his male nurse, many suspect that his death was due to his cooperation with the FBI and Swiss authorities.

It is important to note that three days after the $4.8 billion was transferred to Safra's bank, the Russian Central Bank defaulted on most of its short term debt and the financial crash ensued. During the following chaos, it is alleged that Safra was instructed by the Russian Central Bank and Russian Ministry of Finance to move the funds quickly into other foreign accounts through a complex series of international transfers. Safra subsequently explained to the FBI the mechanisms that Russians had been using to launder money through American Banks.

As mentioned, there are some important questions to be asked. Certainly American banking regulations were broken, but from the proceeds of crime aspect, one has to consider what crime has been committed. Obviously the use of accounts to launder revenue from drugs, terrorism, prostitution, blackmail and so on are important, but some laws such as currency controls are only relevant locally. Should a Russian businessman find a loophole that enables him to get hard currency out of Russia to a safer financial environment, are those funds dirty money? The Russians have a $2,000 daily limit that they can transfer out and some businesses have admitted that for payment of a small commission they have been allowed to use the BENEX facility to facilitate moving larger sums. Many call this movement of funds Capital Flight. So, going back to the debate of whether such funds are the proceeds of crime, the risk remains that the criminals will also use such a system as BENEX to move their funds, thus creating a mix of capital flight and criminal funds and it all becomes dirty money.

Subsequent FBI investigations have uncovered nine bank accounts through which some $10 billion was laundered for the Russian mafia who allegedly have connections with the Yeltsin family.

The US are more pro-active than most jurisdictions and they currently claim that Russian crime gangs have infiltrated many Western banks and securities firms to help launder their funds. So keep a watch for the sudden change in lifestyle of employees working in at-risk positions.

Some experts have, in the wake of this case, claimed that British money laundering laws are weak and useless as the USA has mandatory reporting of large transactions, whereas the UK puts that responsibility on the financial institution. Insider Trading was made illegal in the USA 50 years before it became an offence in the UK and their stance is certainly more bullish. Britain invented the term 'offshore' and it is rather interesting that the first known reference to such a facility in the sense of an unregulated financial centre referred not to sun soaked islands somewhere, but the City of London.

The Russians

The break up of the Soviet Union has resulted in the emergence of numerous criminals operating world-wide criminal organisations involved in drug trafficking, arms smuggling, money laundering and every other type of crime known to man on a very large scale.

Four of these criminals claimed to be in the forefront of this activity are Sergei Mikhailov, Grigory Loutchansky, Semion Mogilevitch and Gregory Lerner.

Loutchansky is involved in the black market in nuclear materials, selling fissile materials to Iran and North Korea, selling scud missiles to Iraq, and controls some 40 companies in the West plus some 60 in the former Soviet Union.

Mikhailov gained control of the Russian Exchange Bank, contributed to the Russian banking system taking the money laundering sink title from Panama by 1995, and controls two assassination squads.

Lerner, currently in prison in Israel, set up a bank in Cyprus to launder Russian crime, Italian mafia and Colombian drug money.

Mogilevitch is also involved in arms trading, prostitution, art smuggling, drug trafficking, extortion and money laundering with a Channel Island connection. He holds a graduate degree in Economics from the University of Lvov, and has been described as the most powerful mobster in the world. It is alleged that he controls all freight shipped through Moscow's international airport and is believed to have purchased a bankrupt Asian airline.

At some stage in his criminal career, he became involved in oil and gas, all of the business being passed through a company registered in Alderney, Arbat International. A partner in crime with Mikhailov, who it is also alleged to have Channel Island links, Mogilevitch soon opened another Alderney company, Arigon. Law enforcement agencies established that he was involved with shipping toxic waste from the USA to Chernobyl, stolen art moved through Western auction houses, the operation of a jewellery factory in Hungary to produce counterfeit money, financial instruments and Faberge eggs, plus the establishment of a chain of night clubs called Black and White where he could push prostitutes, drugs and laundered money. In 1995 he became involved in a massive scam.

A Russian engineer had started a magnet manufacturing company in the USA called YBM. Mogilevitch had also started a magnet company called Magnex Rt. The engineer's brother David Bogatin had been involved in a Mafia fuel tax fraud in New York, had fled to Vienna, then on to Poland where he ended up owning a bank, the First Commercial Bank of Lubin. which was set up as a money laundering sink for anyone prepared to pay the fees. He met Mogilevitch.

Mogilevitch decided to set up a shell company called Pratecs which he floated on the Alberta Stock Exchange. YBM and Magnex Rt were merged into this company. He reversed shares in Arbat and Arigon and set up a chain of shell companies in Hungary through which he intended to use the YBN Magnex consortium to launder money. The Pratec books were rigged so that the initial penny share rose in value so fast that the company soon became one of the TSE300 on the exchange.

In 1995, shares were suspended after it was rumoured someone in the company was under investigation. The company claimed that the allegations were related to two UK companies and the lawyers acting for those companies and were not related to YBM or its subsidiary Arigon. As Arigon used the same solicitors and the company under suspicion was owned by an employee and former director of Aragon, they had been unfortunately linked with the investigation. The amazing thing is that everyone in Canada believed them.

The company then announced that it had discovered a new process during the manufacture of magnets called neodymium, which could, allegedly, reduce the cost of refining crude oil. It was also announced that they were purchasing crude oil on the spot market, treating it with this new discovery and selling the treated product to the Ukraine Government under a long term contract. YPM Magnex's sales had quadrupled, net income had jumped to an all time high and share prices went all the way up to $20.15 by March 1998. The company valuation was $1 billion.

Crumax Magnetics was set up as a UK subsidiary and this company controlled Crusteel Magnetics in Sheffield, plus two Lancashire based magnet firms. However the company's statutory auditors Deloitte & Touche were unhappy with the accounts, with no paperwork to back up accounting entries. These accounts showed an increase in YBM's turnover from $90 million in 1996 to $138 million in 1997. YBM claimed that most of the magnets were sold in the USA when in fact they were being shipped to Russia and the Ukraine.

The rumours started, the auditors refused to sign off the accounts, the share price slipped to $14.35 and then the US headquarters of YPM was raided by various law enforcement agencies. The share trading was halted and shareholders were left with $635 million of worthless stock.

In the UK, as mentioned previously, the managing director of Arigon was under the magnifying glass as he was suspected of laundering money through London. The authorities were able to link this man, Konstantin Karat, Arigon and Arbat to Mogilevitch and that they were laundering funds for him. However, the big surprise was that the men doing the laundering were two English solicitors, Adrian Bernard Churchward and Peter Blake-Turner of a small practice called

Blakes. These two had set up the Alderney companies, Arbat and Arigon, plus other Channel Islands companies, Createbury Limited and Limegold Limited. It was discovered that Mogilevitch and Churchward were linked with a company called Pendosi, and that Churchward's wife was Russian and was the mother of Mogilevitch's son.

The South East Regional Crime Squad report makes interesting reading with the conclusion – 'there is no money laundering identification system in existence at Blakes.'

The Police enquiries continued and they were positive that the two solicitors were laundering money for Mogilevitch's criminal activities through the Royal Bank of Scotland, Lombard Street, London. It appeared that as the money was hidden in the solicitor's client accounts, none of the transactions were examined by the bank's money laundering reporting officers. They had, it appeared, to have assumed that the Law Society were responsible for looking into client's accounts for dirty money. The bank were also aware that whenever solicitors are asked about client accounts, the stock answer is client/solicitor privilege. In other words, let's wipe our hands of the matter. It was concluded that in three years, some $50 million was laundered through the client accounts for Mogilevitch. Arigon appeared to be his private company and Arbet the laundry. Neither company appeared to be trading but sums were moving through Arigon and then in and out of Arbet and a funeral business in Moscow.

Churchward, his wife and Blake-Turner were arrested, and search warrants identified extensive intelligence relating to financial transactions by the Mogilevitch organisation. The Royal Bank of Scotland held just over $2 million in three separate Arigon accounts. Warrants for the arrest of Mogilevitch and Karat were issued but lack of cooperation from Moscow meant that the original charges of conspiracy to handle stolen goods was withdrawn and a lesser charge of money laundering offence was considered. However, under the 1993 laws, the clause that they could have used only applied to new clients. The three were released from bail and paid costs.

The Police enquiries continued and they traced $3.2 million that a Russian, Myskinov, had defrauded out of Moscow City government in an advanced fee scam, through the accounts of Pendosi and Createbury. This money had been wired to a Lithuanian Bank, from there to a Hungarian Bank, to accounts held by a Swiss bank at Chemical Bank, New York, onto several accounts in Europe including one controlled by Mogilevitch's associate Mikhailov. Some of the money was then traced from the Channel Islands to the USA to accounts controlled by a Josef Bogatin. They had found YBM. A visit to their offices revealed a room in an old schoolhouse in Pennsylvania.

It was then discovered that Pratecs was being listed on the Alberta exchange and despite warnings from the British Police and FBI, the company was floated with the consequences previously mentioned.

The only satisfaction that the Police had was the closure of all of Mogilevitch's companies and bank accounts. He was also banned from entering the UK and USA.

However, days after the raid on YBM Magnex, Arigon resurfaced in the Cayman Islands under the name United Trade Limited. Forensic accountants have since discovered a web of mysterious bank accounts, unexplained money transfers and unusual transactions. In other words – money laundering. These apparently involve millions of dollars.

To sum up, the Regional Crime Squad and NCIS conclude that YBM Magnex was formed for a single purpose, 'to legitimise the Mogilevitch criminal organisation by the floating in the stock exchange of a corporation which consists of the UK and USA companies whose existing assets and stocks have been artificially inflated by the introduction of the proceeds of crime.'

The other system used by the Russians is 'Tolling' or transfer pricing. Under this scheme, the Russian company sell products at below market prices to an offshore intermediary. The product is then sold at the market price and the foreign currency proceeds never enter Russia.

I mentioned the sale of nuclear materials earlier and it is worthy of comment that the old USSR military constructed 132 nuclear bombs contained in suitcases. To date only 48 can be accounted for. With the lack of pay to military staff, the widespread corruption and links between the Russian Mafia, The Triads and other organised crime, and the current political unrest in certain parts of the world, one can only but guess as to whether any of these devices are being offered to whoever can meet the asking price.

As I proof-read this book, a journalist in Moscow has telephoned requesting assistance in the investigation of cash received for bribes in respect of Russian Government construction contracts. Whether this is the alleged transfer of funds to an Isle of Man Bank to an Isle of Man registered company, via Switzerland and on behalf of an associate of President Putin, I do not know. No doubt another chapter in the history of money laundering is about to unfold.

The Triads

Whereas the Colombians control the cocaine market, the Triads are the main criminal syndicates behind the heroin market with 60% of the world's supply coming from the Golden Triangle in Burma, Thailand and Laos. This supply is controlled mainly by the Teochiu Triad who have apparently been in the drugs business since 1875 -what one could claim to be a well-established business. The Teochiu are the world's largest ethnic grouping of Chinese expatriates with their own global underground banking system whose money launderers are claimed to be the most skilled in the world with an excellent business management structure. The Teochiu own politicians and lawyers throughout South East Asia with links to the Tiawanese Government, American Mafia, Italian and Russian crime syndicates.

The Triads predate the Roman Empire and were originally known either as 'a hui' (an association) or a 'chaio' (a sect). Various other names were used such as:

> hsieh-chaio – (vicious sects)
> wei-chaio – (false god sects)
> chaio-fei – (bandit sects)
> yin-chaio – (obscene sects)
> yao-chaio – (perverse sects)

Whereas the Triads now deal with heroin, the origination of their drug trafficking was in the import and sale of opium.

In 1994, the World Bank assessed that more money changed hands for drugs than for food, and on that basis, one can assume that Triad income exceeds the gross domestic product of many nations. One of the Teochiu heroin bosses allegedly has HK$980 million deposited in a Chinese bank in Hong Kong. The authorities cannot seize it as such action may cause a run on the bank and many small depositors would face financial ruin. The profits are reinvested in other illegal operations with the bulk being laundered into legitimate businesses.

Another business operation that provides income of some $4 billion dollars a year is the smuggling of illegal immigrants from China. China has some 300 million people (conservative estimate) who are either unemployed or living on the bread-line. Many seek employment overseas and pay the Triad gangs the going rate for transportation by sea or air to Europe or North America. The recent case in the United Kingdom where a large number of Chinese were found dead in a lorry container was undoubtedly part of this business in human misery. It is estimated that there are some 500,000 illegal Chinese immigrants in transit around the world at any given time.

They also operate Cyber Protection Rackets where, by using Denial of Service (DOS) attacks on financial businesses, hold the business to ransom. The Cyber criminals use either High Intensity Radio Frequency (HIRF) guns, Electromagnetic Pulse Cannons (EMP), or Logic Bombs. The first two types of attack weapons were used in the Gulf war to disable Iraqi communication systems and avionics computers and work by firing bursts of electronic power to disrupt computer circuitry and destroy hard disks. Logic bombs are encrypted algorithms hidden in computer systems by sleepers, usually temporary office staff. Activated by a telephone call on a predetermined date, they lock out the computer by encrypting data on the hard disk thus denying access. In other words the computer has been hijacked and the company denied access to its business. An appropriate ransom is demanded on receipt of which a code is given to reverse the encryption.

In London in 1993, two stockbrokers and a merchant bank were blackmailed out of £32.5 million to enable them to regain control of their computers.

Since then, there have been some 60 reported cases with ransoms totalling over £800 million being paid. Of course, many victims do not report the 'incidents' as such bad publicity about their computer security systems is not very welcome.

But perhaps one of the biggest sources of income for the Triad gangs, allied to the use of illegal immigrants, is the revenue obtained from kickbacks in the Far East construction industry. One author estimated that 12% of the construction costs of a Hong Kong skyscraper is written off against kick backs. If one considers that the cost of skyscraper construction is averaging some HK$4 billion, and the Triads take 12% of that on each project, the 'receipts' from each skyscraper are enormous. Extend that revenue across the major cities of the Far East and the amount of criminal revenue is beyond comprehension.

The Triads have linked with Russian organised crime groups and are now recognised as part of the most dangerous organised crime organisations in the world and with some 60 million Chinese living outside of China (this expatriate population being the largest in the World with he exception of the descendants of the African slave trade) the Triads operations are, without doubt, worldwide.

Forgeries

The recent conviction of a counterfeiting gang in the Home Counties identified that their bank-notes were so good that it is estimated that some £30 million are circulating the UK and bent credit cards (usually manufactured in the Far East) cause $1.3 billion worth of fraud each year. It is reported that credit card data is being stolen by dishonest shop and restaurant staff (a double swipe of the card while the customer is not looking), sent to Hong Kong where duplicate cards are forged by the Triads, sold to the Italian Mafia who sell them to Russian criminals where they are used to purchase high quality goods which then finally appear on the shelves at specialist boutiques at the

Gum department store in Moscow.

The Italian Mafia have apparently stockpiled forged euro notes which they plan to flood the market with in 2002 when they are officially introduced.

We have included this intelligence as it identifies more dirty money that will have to enter the legitimate money market. The Mafia have to deposit the cash made from their credit card sales, the retailers have purchased stolen goods and have to account for the purchases somehow, and the forgers have to bank their ill-gotten gains.

How safe are you ?

In the late 1980s, some people entered a US bank located in a known drug trafficking area and conducted a substantial cash transaction. Two senior executives of the bank considered the transaction suspicious so they complied with federal anti-money laundering law and reported the transaction to the US Treasury. (Financial Crimes Enforcement Centre in Washington on a special currency transaction report (CTR)).

The customers had been referred to the bank by a member of its Board of Directors as successful Mexican businessmen. Frequent large cash deposits were made and each were subject of a CTR report sent to FCEC Washington. No official notification was received from FCEC.

Three years later the two executives were arrested and charged with money laundering and providing false and misleading information to the US Treasury. Subsequently, a charge of conspiracy was added by the US Attorney General. However the prosecution evidence was poor and the case collapsed.

However, the trial ruined the bankers' reputations and undermined the creditability of the bank. Their banking careers are ruined and the bank itself is close to financial ruin, yet they had carried out their responsibilities by reporting as required by law. The fact that the customers were drug traffickers was not their concern.

The US has a zero tolerance in respect of money laundering and within its powers, they will extradite and prosecute anyone world-wide who is found to launder funds or monetary instruments that are of dollar $ denomination.

Latest News

Sweet Smelling Money
The New York District Attorney's Office recently announced the arrest of some 40 individuals including three Colombian money brokers. Apparently drugs money was being taken to a perfumery in New York (A & V Perfume World, Herald Square, New York) where is was packaged with perfume and mailed to Colombia. A number of wire transfers to a Tokyo-Mitsubishi account were also discovered, plus half a ton of cocaine and $15 million in cash.

Good Sports
During May 2000, at least two prominent professional sportsmen in the USA have been arrested on money laundering charges, one involved drug trafficking, but the other emphasises our comments about zero tolerance as the individual had used stolen credit cards for defrauding various individuals in a ticket sales scam and the income derived from this theft has been treated by the Federal authorities as money laundering.

FATF Report 22 June 2000
The FATF recently completed a review of anti-money laundering measures to check world-wide effectiveness in various countries and territories. Fifteen jurisdictions were listed as being non-cooperative and failing to comply with the international standards for effective anti-money laundering measures.

The fifteen deemed unsatisfactory are Bahamas, Cayman Islands, Cook Islands, Dominica, Israel, Lebanon, Liechtenstein, Marshall Islands, Nuaru, Niue, Panama, Philippines, Russia, St Kitts and Nevis, St Vincent and the Grenadines. Remember our 'holiday poster' back on page 28?

In addition, a number of countries were identified as failing to meet all of the FATF criteria and Jersey, Guernsey, Isle of Man and Gibraltar were criticised for:

- the use of an 'indirect obligation' to report suspicious transactions related to some criminal offences as opposed to a 'direct obligation' for all predicated offences

- the practice to allow intermediaries to introduce business where the verification of customer identity was an obligation of the introducer instead of the bank

- the lack of a stringent scheme to apply the new rules of customer identification for accounts opened prior to the new rules being introduced.

No doubt the various Financial Services/Supervision Commission will be discussing these criticisms with the FATF in due course.

Summer Holidays?

Since the 1970s, the Costa del Sol has been a sanctuary for British and other European criminals and became renamed the Costa del Crime. Lately things have deteriorated to such an extent that the Spanish law enforcement agencies have developed an elite corps, UDYCO or organised crime units. Basically, Marbella has become the Miami of Europe, with international crime gangs using the area as a base for laundering drugs money which is invested into major construction projects along the coast. Syndicates from Bogota and Moscow are setting up local operations. Gangland killings are frequent and the Spanish now call the area 'La Costa del Plomo' or the lead bullet coast.

Drugs arrive from Morocco for distribution throughout Europe. Russian Mafia have allegedly bribed local politicians and the judiciary, using the area as a 'rest camp' from their activities elsewhere, purchasing real estate, yachts and luxury cars with wads of cash. One yacht, The Joselle, purchased by crooked Moscow banker Alexander Sigarev (he stole £50 million from clients of his collapsed bank, Novbusinessbank) has recently been seized by the Spanish police after the arrest of some 13 men including hit men from Moscow. British crime gangs are dealing with Colombians who have set up cocaine refineries in Malaga, drugs being smuggled across the Straits of Gibraltar.

The police are extremely concerned about the relationship developed by Sigarev with Marbella's notoriously corrupt town hall where he obtained special licences for land around his property. They also claim that the mayor, Jesus Gil, uses Marbella as his own fiefdom merging his business interests with municipal funds. His 'money talks' policy makes the area a haven for drug barons, money launderers and the Mafia.

Operation Lugano

The German Police, working with other agencies, have uncovered a crime ring set up to defraud Germany of $19.6 million in tax receipts through a money laundering network disguised as international cell phone businesses.

Drugs money 3, Soccer O

As previously mentioned, any business that is cash based such as casinos, video rental shops, fast food outlets and so on are ideal scenarios for the laundering of dirty money. The latest businesses to become involved are football clubs. The drug barons have realised that:

- many professional soccer clubs are strapped for cash – (Real Madrid currently operate on a massive multi-million dollar overdraft)
- large sums of money are collected at the turnstiles.
- much of the business in the buying and selling of players is also cash orientated.

We can all remember the cash bungs scandal several years ago where wads of cash was paid to various people to enhance transfers and such like.

Intelligence from NCIS has revealed that syndicates are planning to move large sums of cash to invest in football clubs. Most of the money is the proceeds of drug deals and to date there have been several cases of money launderers and criminals attempting to buy stakes in English and Scottish clubs. Apparently, once an investment has been made they would be able to launder between £10,000 to £20,000 a week by adding the cash to the gate money when banked each week. Other cash can be laundered, as mentioned, during the buying and selling of players.

One can only but speculate on the situation elsewhere in the world with the large gate revenues of some Italian, Spanish and South American soccer clubs, combined with the integrity (?) of the anti-money laundering controls, and, in some cases, ineffective judiciary/law enforcement, in those jurisdictions.

False documents

Following on from the football theme, it now transpires that a number of English Premiership clubs have purchased South American players who, on arrival in the United Kingdom, have been found to have forged passports (Italian and Portuguese). Now we all know that part of 'know your client' is the need for the new customer to produce documents to verify their identity.

As previously mentioned, I recently contacted a West Midland based company where the proprietor offered the facility to open offshore bank accounts anywhere in the world, and more importantly the supply of a passport from whatever jurisdiction one could afford to pay for. The need to ensure that passports and other identification documents or banking instruments are genuine cannot be over-emphasised.

It also transpires that the Portuguese Government admits that several of their European offices have been burgled by the Mafia who they allege have sold passports to various 'clients' including South American soccer players playing for major Italian soccer clubs.

Colombian Navy

It was quite a surprise to find that the drug cartels were building a submarine in a workshop in Bogota. Using American and Russian expertise, the submarine was only partially built when discovered.

The size of the planned vessel, if completed, would have allowed the drug cartels to ship a third of the annual drug production at any given time.

Sani Abacha

The late Nigerian dictator allegedly looted billions of dollars during his rule of what many experts claim is one of the most corrupt countries in the World. Investigators hunting for the missing money have so far discovered some $630 million in Luxembourg banks, the accounts being opened by his sons using false names. Obviously, know-your-client went completely out of the window at those banks. The Swiss Federal Banking Commission reported that a number of leading Swiss Banks had failed to check more thoroughly the origin of the funds allegedly stolen by Abacha (some $4 billion went missing during his 4 years in power).

Similarly millions have been deposited, via Switzerland, at a branch of a European bank in London. The FSA has reported that $126 million was deposited in Jersey banks.

Cash Paid Employees (especially illegals)

A large proportion of the manual field workers employed in the United Kingdom are either illegal immigrants from the old Soviet bloc or those claiming unemployment benefits. These unfortunates are usually paid in cash for obvious reasons.

Some of the proprietors of these 'employment agencies' sometimes called Gangmasters, are known to be unscrupulous and dishonest, running tax avoidance schemes and shell companies to conceal their true income. Obviously, as they pay their staff in cash, they have to withdraw the weekly wages from the bank in cash. However the latest intelligence is that drug dealers have found that this need for cash is an ideal place to 'lose' their dirty money. This drugs money is used to pay the 'employees' and money paid legitimately to the employment agency by the farmer or food processing company is laundered by payments onwards to the drug dealers' front companies.

94

One in five cigarettes smoked in the United Kingdom has been smuggled into the country – Official Sources

Unfortunately that statement is not true, the real figure is nearer one in three. From the piles of dog ends noted outside the various financial institutions in the City of London, a high percentage end up in the square mile. Apparently, offices are visited on a regular basis by cigarette 'vendors' selling proprietary brands at half the normal retail price.

Many of you may have read that The British American Tobacco Company are under investigation by the Department of Trade and Industry into alleged cigarette smuggling. What makes this interesting from a money laundering aspect is that, if one looks at the economics of the extent of the smuggling of cigarettes/tobacco into the United Kingdom and investigates the exports of cigarettes by the major tobacco companies, many of the brands exported to various countries are not retailed in those particular marketplaces. For example, some nine billion cigarettes exported to Cyprus are brands not sold or smoked on that island. These 'exports' are finding their way back to the United Kingdom by the container-load.

Forget the white van driver nipping across the channel to purchase a van load for resale to his or her mates, the economics of container loads are brilliant. A 40-foot container can hold cigarettes with a revenue value of £1 million which have an illegal profit, if smuggled, of £500,000. As mentioned earlier in this book, these smuggled cigarettes end up being sold at car boot sales, in clubs, pubs and in inner city deprived housing projects.

HM C&E have, it is reported, seized some 2 billion cigarettes in 2000, half of which were Imperial Tobacco brands. Unfortunately, they only managed to intercept 10% of smuggled loads which in effect means that 20 billion, with an estimated illegal profit of £1.25 billion, will end up for sale in the United Kingdom. HMC& E have identified what are termed 'export hubs' from where goods are 're-exported' back to the United Kingdom. These hubs include China, Egypt, the Middle East, the Balkans and South Africa. Andorra was on this list with exports to that country increasing from 13 million cigarettes in 1993 to 1.52 billion in 1997. Despite the obvious reason that the Andorrans (population 78,000) increased their daily puff to 55,000 cigarettes or 2,750 packs each per day, their pleas were ignored and the powers to be stopped this activity in 1998 and the smugglers found other more lenient jurisdictions.

HM C&E are equipping themselves with specialised x-ray equipment in an attempt to reduce this smuggling, the cigarettes being hidden in cargoes of furniture and such like. Recently, successful searches identified a road tanker vehicle where the tanker compartments contained cigarettes, not bulk liquid and 'furniture' constructed from cigarette cartons. To date, sniffer dogs have been used but when one is facing examining thousands of containers a day, the use of dogs becomes somewhat time consuming with limited effect.

Some 80% of the smuggled cigarettes are controlled by organised crime who will have to launder their profits.These criminals are the Russian Mafia, Balkan criminal gangs, Greek, South African and Far East crime syndicates. Initially, the cigarettes are exported quite legitimately to wherever (usually an import/export company) who pay the tobacco company for the goods. The shipment is then sold on to various distributors, who then smuggle it in containers back to the United Kingdom where the 'cargo' is distributed to various vendors who sell the goods in pubs etc. Because of this dilution of the profits by each transaction making a profit for the selling party, identification of the dirty money is difficult. In fact it is smurfing in reverse.

Let me explain:

- One – the sale of tobacco to import/export company in X = one container load of 8,000,000 cigarettes or 400,000 packs @£1 per pack = £400,000.

- Two – sold on to crime syndicate for £450,000, making export company £50,000.

- Three – crime syndicate sells to sub-contractors for £500,000, realising a profit of £50,000.

- Four – sub contractors smuggle the cigarettes into the UK where they are sold to vendors at 50% UK price, say at £2 per pack = £800,000. The profit to the sub-contractors is £300,000.

- Five – cigarettes are sold in pubs etc for profits of 20p per pack realising £80,000 split between a large number of street vendors.

- The purchaser still only pays £2.20 as opposed to over £4 per pack.

So the profits are split and only identification of the large bulk profits will identify the smugglers and dirty money.

Transaction examples

The following examples are some of the methods used to hinder identification of the true source of dirty money.

Exchange Bureaux
Drafts obtained from foreign exchange bureaux have frequently been used to open accounts in UK banks. Cash smuggled from the USA into Mexico was placed in exchange bureaux (cambio houses) and drafts purchased. The drafts ranged in value between $5,000 and $500,000. After the UK bank account was opened, the funds were then transferred by wire to another jurisdiction.

It is important to ask the question of how did the UK bank accept the drafts and open the account, especially with money laundering legislation? If the bank did not complete proper vetting, the answer is obvious. Of course, if an existing client opened the account with what appeared to be legitimate documentation, the only indication that there may be something wrong would be the origination of the draft.

Bogus property companies
As mentioned in our detail of the Brinks-Mat robbery, bogus property companies can be used to launder money. Recent investigation into drug traffickers importing cannabis from West

Africa revealed that some of the proceeds were laundered through a bogus company set up in the United Kingdom. A solicitor set up a client account and deposited £500,000 received from the criminals. This was then transferred to his company's bank account. Acting on instructions from the criminals he used the funds to purchase property on their behalf.

Similarly a client of ours was recently approached by an individual wishing to make substantial investments and attempting to back up his status with the fact that he had a Jersey registered property company with massive property investments in the UK. Needless to say, investigation of the Jersey company did not identify any such investments or business.

Money Laundering using cash transactions

There are a variety of 'schemes' that the money launderer will use by converting cash at the placement stage of the laundering process. The following is not a complete list but provides some good examples.

● unusually large cash deposits made by an individual or company whose normal business would be conducted by means of cheques or other instruments

● substantial increases in cash deposits without an apparent cause especially if almost immediately transferred to a destination not associated with the customer

● cash deposited in small amounts by numerous deposits that total a substantial amount (in other words 'smurfing')

● company accounts that show a preponderance of cash transactions where business is normally completed by means of cheques, letters of credit etc

● customers who constantly deposit cash to cover requests for bankers drafts, money transfers etc (the question is – where does the cash come from?)

- customers who change large quantities of low denomination notes for those of a higher denomination as this can indicate the collection of illegal funds from drug dealers where cash is the normal method of trade

- frequent exchange of cash for foreign currencies

- bank branches that have more cash transactions than normal (see our comments re the Lansky Legacy in the Bahamas)

- customers whose deposits include forged currency or instruments (I can recall investigating the activities of a private bank which was known to contravene exchange control laws appertaining to its home base country in Africa (I was investigating alleged money laundering) and forged US currency was discovered in the Bank's safe. Despite being advised that the currency was forged, the owners of the bank failed to report the transaction to the regulatory body.)

- customers transferring large amounts of money to and from overseas locations with instructions for payment in cash

- large cash deposits made using night safe facilities thus avoiding direct contact with bank staff.

Money laundering using bank accounts
The following styles are frequently used.

- customers who wish to maintain a number of trustee or client accounts which do not appear consistent with the type of business, including transactions which involve nominees

- customers who have numerous bank accounts and deposit cash into each account that in accumulative total are substantial (a form of smurfing)

- any individual or company whose account shows no personal or business banking activity yet is used to receive and disburse large sums of money that have no obvious purpose or relationship to the account holder and/or their business – the recently reported case where it is alleged that a confidant of Russian President Putin into a dormant business account at an Isle of Man bank is a good example of this type of transaction

- reluctance to provide normal information when opening an account, providing minimal or fictitious information, or providing information that is difficult and expensive to substantiate

- customers who have accounts with several financial institutions in the same locality and where regular consolidation of funds occurs prior to requests for onward transmission of the funds (another form of smurfing)

- regular payments out of an account that match deposits made the previous day (used by the money launderer to extend the 'audit trail', the transaction usually going, via several other bank accounts elsewhere, to an account in a jurisdiction where bank secrecy laws make investigation difficult)

- depositing large third party cheques endorsed in favour of the customer

- large cash withdrawals from a dormant/inactive account or from an account that receive an unexpected large credit from overseas

- customers who together or simultaneously use separate tellers to conduct large cash or foreign exchange transactions (another form of smurfing)

- greater use of safe deposit facilities and the use of sealed packets deposited and withdrawn (how often do you check the frequency of safe deposit visits to a particular strongbox?)

- company representatives avoiding contact with the bank

- substantial increases in deposits of cash or negotiable instruments by a professional firm or company, using clients' accounts or in-house company or trust accounts, especially if the deposits are promptly transferred between other client, company and trust accounts

- customers who decline to provide information that in normal circumstances would make the customer eligible for credit or other valuable banking services

- insufficient use of normal banking facilities (avoidance of high interest rates for large balances)

- large number of individuals making deposits into the same account without an adequate explanation (more smurfing).

No doubt there are other methods that the money launderer will use to take advantage of slack or poor controls and awareness.

Money laundering using investment related transactions

Some of the money laundering methods used are:

- purchasing of securities to be held by the financial services business in safe custody where this appears to be inappropriate given the customers apparent standing

- back to back deposit/loan transactions with subsidiaries or affiliates of financial services businesses in sensitive jurisdictions such as Liechtenstein

- request by customers for investment management services (either foreign currency or securities) where the source of funds is unclear and not consistent with the customer's apparent standing

- large or unusual settlements of securities in cash form

- buying or selling of a security with no discernible purpose or in circumstances which appear unusual.

Money laundering by offshore international activity
The following examples should be considered as suspicious transactions:

- a customer that has been introduced by an overseas branch, affiliate or other bank based in countries where production of drugs or drug trafficking may be prevalent

- use of Letters of Credit and other methods of trade finance to move funds between countries where such trade is outside the customer's normal trading pattern or business

- customers who make regular and large payments, including wire transfers, that cannot be verified as bona fide transactions to, or regularly receive regular and large payments from, unregulated jurisdictions, especially those with known links to drug trade and terrorism

- accumulation of large balances that are inconsistent with the normal business turnover, that are subsequently transferred overseas

- unexplained electronic fund transfers by customers on an in and out basis or without passing through a financial services product

- frequent requests for traveller's cheques, foreign currency drafts or other negotiable instruments to be issued outside the normal pattern of trade

- frequent deposits of travellers' cheques or foreign currency drafts originating from overseas.

Money laundering involving financial services employees and agents

This area is often overlooked but is important to monitor as an in-house control. The following examples are typical indications:

- a change in employees' characteristics such as lavish lifestyle, and avoiding taking holidays

- changes in an employee's or agent's performance (the salesman selling products for cash has a remarkable or unexpected increase in performance)

- any deal with an agent where the identity of the ultimate beneficiary or counterpart is undisclosed contrary to normal procedures for the type of business

- money laundering by secured and unsecured lending

- customers who repay problem loans unexpectedly

- requests to borrow against assets held by the financial services business or a third party where the origins of the assets are not known or the assets are inconsistent with the customer's status

- request by a customer for a financial service business to provide or arrange finance where the source of the customers financial contribution to a deal is unclear, particularly where property is involved.

Money laundering by sales and dealing staff

1. New Business
Although it may be possible that long-standing clients are laundering money through an investment business, it is far more likely that a new customer will use one or more financial services products for a short period only and they may use false names and fictitious companies.

Investment may be direct with a financial services business or indirect through an intermediary who 'does not ask too many awkward questions', especially (but not only) in jurisdictions where money laundering is not legislated against or where the rules are not rigorously enforced.

We recommend that the following situations will require you to make additional enquiries:

- a person or client where verification of identity proves unusually difficult and who is reluctant to provide details

- a corporate/trust client where there are difficulties and delays in obtaining copies of the accounts or other documents of incorporation

- a client with no apparent reason for using the firm's services such as clients with distant addresses that could find the same service nearer home and those that require services outside the firm's normal trading pattern who could be easily serviced elsewhere

- an investor introduced by an overseas bank, affiliate or other investor both of which are based in unregulated countries or countries known to be involved in the drugs, arms or terrorist trade

- any transaction in which the counterpart to the transaction is unknown.

2. Intermediaries

There are many legitimate reasons for a client's use of an intermediary. However the use of intermediaries introduces further parties into the transaction thus increasing opacity and, depending on the designation of the product, preserving anonymity. Similarly, there are a number of legitimate reasons for dealing via intermediaries on a 'numbered account' basis, but this is also a useful method which may be used by the money launderer to delay, obscure or avoid detection.

Any apparently unnecessary use of an intermediary in the transaction should be investigated.

3. Dealing patterns and abnormal transactions

As mentioned earlier, the aim of the money launderer is to introduce as many layers as possible and this means that the money will pass through a number of sources, different persons and entities. Long standing and apparently legitimate client holdings may be used to launder money innocently, as a favour, or due to the exercise of undue pressure. Examples of unusual dealing patterns and abnormal transactions are:

Dealing Patterns

- a large number of security transactions across a number of jurisdictions

- transactions not in keeping with the investor's normal activity, the financial markets in which the investor is active and the business which the investor operates

- buying or selling of a security with no discernible purpose or in circumstances which appear unusual, e.g. 'churning' at the client's request

- low grade securities purchased in an overseas jurisdiction, sold locally and high grade securities purchased with the proceeds

- bearer securities held outside a recognised custodial system.

Abnormal Transactions

- a number of transactions by the same counterpart in small amounts of the same security, each purchased for cash and then sold in one transaction, the proceeds being credited to a product different from the original (e.g. a different account)

- any transaction in which the nature, size or frequency appears unusual, e.g early termination of packaged products at a loss due to front end loading; early cancellation especially where cash has been tendered and/or the refund cheque is to a third party

- transfer of investments to unrelated third parties

- transactions not in keeping with normal practice in the market to which they relate, e.g. with reference to market size and frequency, or at off-market prices

- other transactions linked to the transaction in question which could be designed to disguise money and to divert it into other forms or other destinations or beneficiaries.

Money laundering by settlements

1. Payment

The money launderer will usually have substantial amounts of cash to dispose of and will, as mentioned earlier, use a variety of sources to deposit the money. Cash settlement through a financial adviser or broker may not in itself be suspicious, however large or unusual settlements of securities deals in cash and settlements in cash to a large securities house will usually provide cause for further enquiry. Examples of unusual payment settlement are:

- a number of transactions by the same counterparty in small amounts of the same security, each purchased for cash and then sold in one transaction

- large transaction settlement by cash

- payment by way of cheque or money transfer where there is a variation between the account holder/signatory and the customer.

2. Registration and delivery

Settlement by registration of securities in the name of an unverified third party should prompt further investigation.

Bearer securities, held outside a recognised custodial system, are very portable and anonymous instruments which may serve the purposes of the money launderer well. Their presentation in settlement or as collateral should always prompt further enquiry, as should the following:

- settlement to be made by way of bearer securities from outside a recognised clearing system

- allotment letters for new issues in the name of the persons other Than the client.

3. Disposition

As explained, money laundering is the cleaning of dirty money so that the clean funds can then be used by the criminal to invest in either legitimate business or further criminal enterprise. They need to remove the clean money from the jurisdiction where it is deposited and conceal the destination of those funds.

The following situations should provoke further enquiries:

- payment to a third party without any apparent connection with the investor

- settlement either by registration or delivery of securities to made to an unverified third party

- abnormal settlement instructions including payment to apparently unconnected parties.

Money laundering by e-mail and smart cards

The world wide web or internet is probably the fastest growing communication system ever, being used by commerce and the public to communicate, sell and purchase every type of commodity, and as a leisure tool. Currently there are 12.8 million host locations and 70 million+ users.

With this growth has been the development of electronic money transfers, particularly e-cash which will reduce the need for currency smuggling. The physical bulk of cash has been the main impediment to the money launderer, but new electronic systems can move vast amounts of money instantaneously and securely with a few computer key strokes. The speed of these transactions will hamper identification or tracking by the law enforcement agencies. It is estimated that there will be an e-cash market of some $10 billion worldwide by 2006 and the internet is already being used to perpetrate a wide variety of financial fraud.

Numerous countries are experimenting with e-cash as a replacement for traditional money, particularly the Scandinavian markets and, although it may liberate the economic markets and enhance personal privacy, it will pose a huge problem to those combating money laundering and organised crime.

E-cash owes its existence to three important developments:

- the legal authorisation to convert paper money into electronic data capable of transmission by electronic networks
- the internet
- increased confidence in payment systems through internet and e-mail systems, and increasingly on the internet.

These developments enable the transfer from a paper-based system to an electronic system. Unlike the inter-bank SWIFT system that only allows inter-bank money transfers, e-cash will permit secure electronic payments across the internet to all interested parties. The system is designed to link existing bank networks, merchants and customers worldwide to allow for global transactions. It allows merchants to obtain authorisation on-line and issue electronic receipts.

To use the system, the purchaser must first download an electronic wallet (e-wallet) from the site of an e-money issuer (the mint). This usually happens after the user registers with an e-cash supplier and has opened an account. The downloaded wallet can be installed on the user's PC or notebook. They then select a secret authorising number or code that allows digital identification, enabling the secure transfer of money from an e-money mint to the purchaser's e-wallet for spending with merchants.

The legitimate uses of e-cash are endless – on-line shopping, public transport, restaurants and so on – in fact anything that entails payment by cash or cheque. The system offers complete anonymity. Issuing banks do not link the anonymous e-cash numbers to a particular client, thus making it difficult to link payment transactions to the payer. The money launderers can protect themselves with anonymity.

Some experts have claimed that the problems of electronic money laundering are:

- The money laundered is electronic money because the ease of movement and storage of electronic money makes the launderer's task easier.

- The problem that is usually glossed over is – how does it happens that the criminal has a large amount of electronic money? Was it originally in electronic form or was it converted from hard cash?

Mark Bortner presented a paper on the law and the internet at the University of Miami School of Law where he gave the example of laundering drug money by e-cash. He theorises the situation where after smurfing the hard cash, the money is transferred out of the banks to internet banks that accept e-cash. To protect themselves, the drug traffickers keep the transfers below the reportable amount.

Once transferred, the money has become anonymous and untraceable. Whereas the physical smurfing of hard cash deposits is an offence under money laundering legislation, electronic smurfing is difficult to relate to current banking laws as cyberbanks are not necessarily registered or licenced and cybercash is not recognised as entering the marketplace of hard currency, thus affecting monetary supply or policy. Therefore the requirement for the cyberbank to report a suspicious transaction is probably not mandatory (especially if that cyberbank is registered in somewhere like Niue).

In other words, once the e-cash account is established, funds can be transferred from any computer connected to the internet. As Mark Bortner claims, a truly creative, if not paranoid, launderer could access funds via Telnet, the basic command that involves the protocol for connecting to another computer on the internet. The launderer sitting on a beach with his laptop can connect to his internet service provider in the USA or anywhere, and get the leased internet account to contact the bank or banks to transfer funds to wherever. The risk of identification of the launderer is practically zero. E-cash, being anonymous, allows the account holder total privacy to make internet transactions. Thus the bank holding the digital cash, as well as the seller who accepts e-cash, has virtually no means of identifying the purchaser.

As we all know, money is frequently laundered by the purchase of property or expensive items such as cars, aeroplanes and such like. Currently, there are very few vendors selling such items for e-cash so the launderer may still have to revert the money to hard cash at some stage, thus entering the proverbial spotlight of the alert money laundering reporting officer. However once the property market realise that there is money to be made by accepting e-cash, even if there is a mandatory report made by them that they sold a property for £2 million, the investigator will find it difficult to identify the purchaser. Subsequent enquiries may reveal ownership by some Niue-registered shell company, but the subsequent investigation will be difficult. One can only hope that the criminal follows the usual pattern of making a mistake, thus opening the doors to the investigators.

Until the patterns of abuse become apparent, all e-cash transactions should be dealt with extreme caution.

E-cash systems on the market are:

Cyber- Cash	www.cybercash.com
Digicash	www.digicash.com
Ecash, Net Chex	www.netchex.com
Net Cash	www.gost.isi.ed/info/netcash
NetBill	www.ini.cmu.edu/netbill

Mondex	www.mondex.com
Bitbux and VisaCash	www.visa.com

Smart cards are another innovation which may also provide the means for a money launderer to transfer funds without using the normal banking system. If no limit is placed on the amount of money that can be placed on a smart card, the criminal will be able to transfer funds from his card to another card via a computer. Launderers will become free of the two problems they currently face:

- there will be no need to enter the money into the banking system
- there will be no need to carry around bags of cash.

Even street level drugs deals could be completed by using smart cards. Despite conferences and discussion forums being held to discuss the weaknesses in the proposed smart card systems, the current proposals do not appear to have any in-built controls over individual smart card identification (i.e card to registered user) thus stolen cards, or transferred cards will replace cash and an electronic card holding substantial funds that cannot be traced is a better risk than a suitcase of banknotes that needs washing.

Michael Levi, an academic, stated,

The whole idea of a suspicion based system (suspect transaction reporting) is old fashioned, since unlike burglaries and robberies, most cross-border transactions are conducted purely electronically, without anyone physically seeing them: because of the legislation (and sometimes to guarantee that the transaction will be paid for) customers must be identified, but how are the bankers to know whether there is legitimate business case for the myriad transactions they undertake, and why should it be their business to 'shadow' their customers? Legislation does not require them to do these things, but they (and the 'informal banking' sector) would have to do so if they were to smoke out all the laundering and fraud.

In Australia, there is a central system called AUSTRAC that is basically a computer forensic programme that looks for trends and patterns of electronic transfers thus enabling automated collection of objective data rather than the reliance of the subjective human judgment of bank tellers and their supervisors. Some experts are looking at self-regulation by the use of tailor-made detection systems that forensically examine transactions and only highlight those that are suspicious, thus eliminating those that are currently reported because of human interaction, when in fact they are quite innocent.

NCIS use a forensic analysis system to identify links between various individuals and companies but that system uses the suspicious incident reports as input data.

In October 2000, the US government enacted legislation that made an electronic signature valid in law with the same status as a written signature. Some experts claim that this law will make it easier for criminals to perpetrate fraud by theft of identity. Others claim that technological advances will make it more difficult to steal identities. It will be imperative the customer has appropriate software protection with encrypted digital signatures, such as a public key kept by a third party that guarantees that the key belongs to the individual, and a private key which is kept secret by the user/customer. However, this new marketplace will still require customer verification if money laundering is to be avoided. One company director whose company sells encryption technology to banks claims that investors will soon be able to sell stocks direct to each other, thus eliminating stockbrokers. The mind boggles and one wonders how the regulatory bodies will be able to legislate and control such trade.

There is no doubt that the whole area of electronic banking is open to abuse by the money launderer and, as I write this manual, an internet bank, and possibly others, has been hit with an attempted alleged industry-wide fraud by organised crime where the creation of multiple false loans, bank and credit cards on-line had taken place. Fortunately, the bank had crested software to identify multiple account applications which use false details. Anyone, according to current experience, making a false application usually uses the same address or employment and uses the same computer terminals. This type of control is essential when one considers the basic anti-money laundering rule of 'Know your Client'. I have no doubt that the clever criminal will overcome this problem by using corrupt individuals or companies as smurfs to launder their dirty money. The anonymity of the internet will help keep the money hidden.

Money laundering systems

In the previous chapters, we have detailed some case examples of how the criminal launders money through the world's banking systems and constantly looks for new ways and new technology to aid the legitimisation of his dirty money.

One system that has been very difficult to investigate is the Asian and Chinese underground banking systems. The Asian system is known as Hawallah and is based on a family concept using a world-wide network of ethnic Pakistani and Indian families providing efficiency and confidentiality for those wishing to avoid conventional banking channels.

Hawallah means 'reference' in Hindi, or 'transfer related money' in Arabic, and 'trust' in Urdu. The system is also called 'Chop' or 'Hundi' or by the Chinese 'fei ch'ien' which means flying money (see earlier comments in respect of the Triads).

The funds are layered through a complex chain of wire transfers, gold smuggling, and invoice manipulation. They are then usually integrated into legitimate business or investment in real estate.

The main elements of the Hawallah system are:

Confidentiality
This is crucial between client and the hawallah dealer and a code of silence governs all transactions with dire consequences attached to the breach of trust. Should the code be broken, the dealer would put not only his business, but his life in jeopardy.

Convenience
Hawallah dealers often operate in rural areas of under-developed

countries where there are no conventional banking services, and the dealer fills this void. They offer the same services as provided by conventional banks, such as cashier's cheques, money orders and currency exchange. Even where conventional banks exist, it is not uncommon to have hawallah dealers working as tellers.

Efficiency

Banking transactions through the normal banking channels, especially in third world countries, can be slow and complex. However the hawallah system can transfer large sums of money internationally within hours with little or no paperwork and no physical movement of funds.

The established, well known families who operate the hawallah systems have earned a great deal of trust and respect within their communities. Many operate legitimate businesses with substantial cash flow and include travel agencies, carpet companies, gold dealerships, gem trading companies. Family members or associates of the same ethnic or religious group operate similar sister companies in foreign cities where there are large Indian or Pakistani communities.

Cost Effectiveness

The economic incentive to use the hawallah system rests upon favourable exchange rates and the low cost of hawallah transactions. The exchange rate used in the hawallah system is based on the Indian black market dollar price which is linked to the amount of gold being smuggled into the country. Therefore the exchange rate offered can be 10-25% better than the official exchange rate. It has been estimated that $10 billion a year passes through the Hawallah system in India.

The hawallah dealer provides better rates and charges lower commissions because he makes additional profits through speculation in the money markets with the remittance funds and holds those funds in interest bearing accounts prior to transfer.

Operation

The most common method of hawallah dealing is for the client who wishes to transfer funds overseas in secret to go to the hawallah dealer who will agree the commission and exchange rate and take the cash from the client. This cash is usually in the currency of the client's home country. These funds are deposited locally by the hawallah dealer being intermingled with the dealer's legitimate business.

The client is given a chit. This may be half of a playing card, a banknote or marked scrap of paper. During a money laundering investigation several years ago, I was searching the offices of an Asian accountant in London and in one of the desks found numerous blank sheets of paper all having been signed by customers in India. Obviously these pre-signed sheets enabled the accountants to write instructions to whoever to comply with their client's wishes. This of course would include money transfers, payments and so on.

During the Vietnam war, hawallah dealers cashed American GIs' pay cheques at a favourable rate of exchange, sent the cheques to their opposite numbers in New York where the cheques were cashed, the cash then used to purchase gold which was then smuggled back to Vietnam and sold on the black market at a very good exchange rate realising good profits.

When the client's agent goes to the hawallah dealer's opposite number in the country where the funds are to be sent, the agent produces the chit and it is matched to the other half by the hawallah dealer. The funds, less the commission, are then paid to the agent.

Hawallah dealers maintain constant reconciliation accounts with other dealers, balances being settled by using Swiss bank accounts and interbank transfers again using the cover of legitimate business activity.

VIETNAM - HAWALLAH DEALS

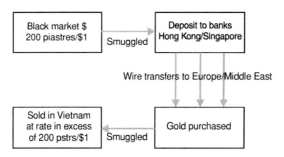

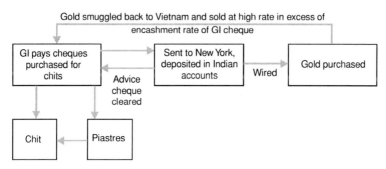

3

Detection

With the ever increasing focus on money laundering throughout the United Kingdom, Channel Islands, Isle of Man and Gibraltar as well as the USA, EC and so on, there has been an increase in the sale of in-house training packages, including a number of computer-based training modules that staff can use to learn how to recognise the suspicious. In addition there has been a proliferation of money laundering seminars. The problem is to sort out the good from the bad. Being the eternal cynic, I do not believe that staff can be trained to recognise the suspicious transaction without the help of well planned systems. The Bank of New York case involved some 160,000 wire transfers over a short period of time. How on earth can anyone be expected to identify one suspicious transaction in so many? I have detailed in this chapter some of the controls and support systems that are available to help with the implementation of anti-money-laundering measures.

Suspicious Wire Transfers

Fortunately, some computer software designers have formulated systems that, by using customer history patterns, will identify the suspicious transaction, and any financial institution dealing with a large client base and associated money movements should consider using this type of software. Basically, the system installed on the bank's computer constantly scans the transactions passing through the various client accounts. Should a transaction fall outside the accepted customer trading/transaction pattern, the transaction is highlighted for investigation. The systems can also identify those multiple transactions that together may prove 'suspicious'.

Some of these systems are very expensive, but the cost should be assessed against the risk of handling dirty money and if not discovered, the potential financial penalties and loss of reputation. Many of the financial jurisdictions insist that there are controls in place to identify the suspicious transaction and if your business handles thousands of transactions, it is obvious that a computerised system is necessary to act as an appropriate filter. One of the leaders in this field are Americas Software in Florida, but there are others in the marketplace. There are also specialist contractors who can also examine data and can formulate procedures to identify suspicious transactions. I would certainly recommend that the prudent financial manager explore the use of such systems and/or forensic computer system specialists.

Should the cost of such systems be too high, I would recommend the smaller business should consider setting up a joint facility with other similar businesses, thus sharing the cost. I realise that such an arrangement may be against all client confidentiality agreements, but the data could easily be encoded so that the joint facility or bureau merely reports back to the appropriate participating financial institution the coded suspicious transaction report for decoding and subsequent reporting or investigation.

Office of Foreign Assets Control – (OFAC)

As discussed elsewhere in this book, the Americans are more bullish than most in respect of money laundering where their currency is involved. Whereas one could argue that drugs trafficking is mainly an American problem and that there are too many coke-heads in California, it is important that one recognises that the launderer will seek other jurisdictions and 'friendly' financial institutions to launder their dirty money. Added to their own internal laws and the fact that they will go anywhere in the world to prosecute those that launder greenbacks, they have also various acts of Congress that empowers OFAC to freeze assets and impose sanctions. OFAC has a blacklist of countries, companies and individuals where they will freeze and impound dollar transactions should such a transaction to any of those on the blacklist be noted. In simple terms, this means that should an honest customer of your bank request a dollar transfer to some freight company in what appears to be a non-suspicious jurisdiction, it is possible that the freight company may be on OFAC's blacklist. So when the dollars go through the American corresponding bank they have a good chance of being frozen by OFAC.

The blacklist is available to Financial institutions on CD-Rom, is updated frequently from FBI/CIA sources and includes details of individuals (including known passports) front companies for terrorist and drug organisations, and countries that the USA and United Nations have sanctions against. Certainly, if your client base includes a reasonable percentage of US dollar transactions, the use of this intelligence is important to protect your clients' funds. In addition, utility programs are available that filter your accounts and transactions before they are sent overseas thus highlighting potential risk transactions.

False Documents and Instruments

The use of computers, digital photography, scanners, and colour laser printing has made forgery a science available to many. As mentioned previously, passports, educational qualification certificates, and other dubious documents can easily be purchased on the web.

So how can the financial institution identify false documents or instruments? Again, it is impossible for the employee to identify such forgeries unless the forgery was obviously prepared using a John Bull printing kit. There are a number of forensic companies who, using the latest technology, can by various tests, establish the validity of a document, whether it be the identity of the printing ink and paper used, the integrity of the watermark or of any evidence of physical or chemical interference. For example, brake fluid is used to remove ink handwriting or rubber stamp marks. This is an old trick which I first came across when investigating MOT/Insurance fraud where out-of-date certificates were immersed in brake fluid to remove the ink handwriting so that new data could be written on the document.

Identification of the paper may prove that the particular type of paper was not produced at the time the alleged document was prepared. The infamous Jack the Ripper and Hitler Diaries were forensically examined to prove or disprove their authenticity. Similarly, certain inks may have been unavailable when the document(s) were written/printed and fingerprint or DNA tests may indicate possible interference by suspects.

Other Forensic Technology

In addition, signatures can be analysed, tape recordings of deals can be enhanced (I used this type of forensic service in a case where an independent foreign exchange dealer claimed that the deals that had gone wrong had not been made on his instruction, but by the bank acting independently on their own volition – by enhancing the back office tapes, we proved he was lying), video security tapes can similarly be enhanced and such technology is frequently used to provide evidence of an incident whether it be the failure to carry out an operation correctly or to identify a crime being committed.

There are also forensic companies that specialise in computers and, using systems designed for law enforcement agencies, they can, without damaging the evidence on a computer, locate deleted or hidden data. These systems can find those documents prepared by the dishonest or devious employee for personal gain. This type of equipment was used when we investigated an industrial espionage case where a director was selling industrial secrets to Japanese competitors. The first document we found was a deleted memo sent by the director to his Japanese contact. In the financial world, such forensics can trace computer data relating to unauthorised transactions that may have been deleted by the dishonest employee.

There is one very important message (unless you are an experienced computer forensic specialist) when you suspect any type of computer fraud or that a computer has been used for dishonest processes – unplug the suspect computer(s) and store in a secure environment or you may lose valuable evidence.

Employment Vetting

This leads to an area where some of the major problems in respect of money laundering lie, pre-employment and ongoing staff vetting. The money launderer has the attitude that some expense is necessary to enable them to launder the money. As I write this book, amongst the latest news mentioned is that the Colombian drug cartels, working with Russian Mafia members and others, have been building a submarine to use for the shipment of drugs into the United States. I await more details with interest. No doubt it was to be fitted with nuclear weaponry provided by the Russians to see off any law enforcement agencies that may have had the cheek to try and stop their voyages.

So the cost of bribing an employee is negligible in the scheme of things. At a fraud and money laundering seminar we held in Jersey, a senior police officer (in his opening address) highlighted the risks and problems of staff dishonesty, especially in the financial environment where staff are frequently transient and can exploit lack of vetting to their personal advantage. It is no use just vetting staff prior to their walking through your front door if the current incumbents are taking money out of the back door by accepting bribes. The question is whether you are aware of changes in employee lifestyle or addictions to gambling, drugs, alcohol, sex or whatever. So often I have investigated fraud and on the successful completion of the investigation the losers have made to me such classic comments as:

'I wondered how he could afford that holiday in the Seychelles.'
'He was always on the phone to the bookies.'
'He changes his cars for new more expensive models every year.'
'He is only a clerk yet his house and its upkeep must cost him thousands.'
'I don't believe it – she is a member of my family.'

Whereas some individuals have other sources of income or may have won the lottery, the majority live within their financial limits. The dishonest will usually flaunt their wealth in one way or another.

It is an interesting fact that one in four job applications are fraudulent and employee vetting has to be more than just taking out references. If an individual is prepared to lie to obtain employment, they may well be prepared to accept bribes to act dishonestly. The dishonest recruit may be either susceptible to bribery and/or corruption or be an experienced fraudster who has targeted your company.

There are a number of important facts to consider in respect of employment vetting:

- 30% of the cost of crime in the retail industry is due to employee dishonesty
- the dishonest applicant could be underqualified, fraudulent and dangerous
- if underqualified, this could mean not only poor performance but negligence
- people who have successfully lied will probably lie again
- long term consequences include bad publicity, industrial espionage, computer crime and low morale

It is important that the employer does not see pre-employment screening as the end of the need for vetting. Vetting in situations of promotions to high risk positions, and monitoring of staff lifestyle are essential management controls. Certainly there is a need to define the sensitivity of the various job positions in your organisation. Consideration should be given to:

- the potential damage to your organisation through fraud, sabotage, or dishonesty
- highest position attainable
- data which may debar employment or promotion
- legal agreements necessary
- agency or temporary staff

However you complete employee vetting, it is essential that you check original documents, not copies. A check must be made of consistency in employment, lack of details, gaps or discrepancies in the chronology of employment history, omissions, wording of statements and eligibility for employment.

In today's computer-related world, there are various databases that can provide details of an individual's background such as electoral roll, credit history, directorships and press articles. In addition, Land Registry, regulatory bodies, P45s and telephone directory enquiries can provide additional material.

Use specialist agencies for comprehensive employee screening but ensure that they are both reputable and experienced.

Training

Staff training is mandatory and different organisations either implement in-house training or use training organisations. Many of these programmes are excellent and include staff role-playing in various scenarios. Certainly examine the marketplace and select the best training programme that suits your needs. Unfortunately, I have found that frequently there is a blinkered approach to staff training. The usual response when invited to conferences where the latest trends and protective systems are to be related to the delegates is:

- we have our own training programme
- we know all we need to know
- we will stick with .... for our training needs

I find that these responses indicate a blinkered approach and perhaps an indication of doing only what one needs to do to meet the minimum requirements as a reactive rather than proactive stance and a failure to face facts. Some of the organisations offering training have little or no investigative experience and it is very important to keep abreast of trends, new protective systems, and who is out there to help you.

Whoever is used should be vetted and be the right organisation for the job. Just because the prospective training provider is a big named company does not necessarily make them the best for the job.

Conclusion

I am not saying that one should try to become an ace investigator but one should accept that in-house resources and experience needed to cope with the problems of money laundering and fraud are rarely fully available and even the in-house security professional will need to seek expert assistance from outside the organisation. Certainly the use of these experts is recommended if the need arises.

4

The Law

Evolution of money laundering laws

Until the 1980s, only a handful of jurisdictions had criminalised money laundering, but as it became obvious that something needed to be done to protect the financial stability of the United States and other countries, the last ten years have seen an increase in the enaction of laws and regulations. As mentioned earlier, money laundering can have a detrimental effect on the social fabric of a country and its national security as the facility to launder dirty money enables the criminal to expand his activities whether it be drug trafficking, terrorism, illegal arms trading, blackmail or fraud.

The USA were the first to enact anti-money laundering laws with any transaction over $10,000 being the subject of mandatory examination. This resulted in 'smurfing' by the criminals to disguise the deposits. Even with the enactment of these laws, many financial institutions in the USA only paid lip service to them, and it was only when very large fines were imposed by the Federal Courts did they sit up and take notice.

The G-7 Nations implemented the Financial Action Task Force (FATF) in 1989 who are now the major driving force promoting action against money laundering, their 40 recommendations being the standard against which anti-money-laundering regimes are measured. Some 26 member jurisdictions are participants of the action plan.

Other multilateral regional groups such as the Organisation of American States, the Caribbean Action Task Force, the Asia/Pacific money laundering within their regions.

Since 1990, various jurisdictions have created Financial Intelligence Units (FIU) who process information received and pass the information on to the appropriate law enforcement agency. To act as a forum for the various FIUs to network with each other and solve common problems, the Egmont Group was formed, and the Egmont Secure Web enables FIUs to communicate securely over the internet. To date, 38 jurisdictions meet the Egmont definition of an FIU, and that includes the United Kingdom, Channel Islands, and Isle of Man. 22 of these FIUs are connected to the secure web.

So the various financial regulatory bodies laid down regulations for the financial businesses to abide by, these regulations being associated with existing and, in some cases, new criminal laws.

UK Regulations

In the United Kingdom, the money laundering regulations were linked to various criminal statutes such as the **Drug Trafficking and Prevention of Terrorism Acts**. For example, Section 1(1) of the Prevention of Terrorism Act includes the power to order forfeiture of any money or property for the use of the terrorist organisation and includes the offence of providing aid in the provision of services. Therefore it is clear that the provision of financial services is contrary to the Act and handling funds belonging to a terrorist organisation would constitute an offence.

The existing laws on money laundering can be found in:

- The Criminal Justice Act 1988
- The Prevention of Terrorism (temporary provisions) Act 1989
- The Criminal Justice Act 1994
- The Drug Trafficking Act 1994
- The Criminal Law (Consolidation) (Scotland) Act 1995
- The Proceeds of Crime (Northern Ireland) Order 1996
- The Money Laundering Regulations 1993 (Regulation 2 (3) defines money laundering and Regulation 14(d) requires the reporting of all offences of suspected money laundering)

I recently read a draft for a 'money laundering book' written by lawyers. It was excellent in content from a legal point of view but quite honestly, unless one is acting as a lawyer to find ways of interpreting the various laws based on stated cases and other legal arguments, the whole concept of what the law really means gets lost in a legal fog.

You know what I mean – we have seen it all before. ('I say, old boy – clause six, subsection two of the 78 Act must mean, if one takes Mickey Mouse v Goofy, blah blah blah …') The application of the legislation, laws and regulations should be based on the simple concept that **as a financial institution you do not wish to handle the proceeds of any criminal activity whatever that activity is.**

If you do, you are no better than the old fashioned fence and your business is profiting from criminal enterprise. The Courts usually take the stance that without 'receivers' there are 'no thieves' so the more difficult it is for the criminals to get their money into your organisation, the better.

In simple terms these various Acts can be summarised as follows:

● It is an offence to conceal, etc, another's proceeds of drug trafficking, terrorism or other criminal acts, knowing or having reasonable grounds to suspect that they are such proceeds.

● It is an offence to enter in an arrangement which facilitates the retention or control by or on behalf of another of their proceeds of crime, or which allows the other's proceeds of crime to be used to secure funds or be used to obtain benefit to acquire property by way of investment, knowing or suspecting that the person concerned is, or has been, involved in criminal activity or has benefited from criminal activity.

● It is an offence to acquire, possess, or use another's proceeds of criminal activity, knowing that they are such proceeds.

➡ **Conviction on indictment for the above offences is punishable by up to 14 years imprisonment, or a fine, or both.**

- It is an offence to fail to report knowledge or suspicions of criminal money laundering or the control of criminal funds to either the Police or a supervisor in accordance with an employer's established system.

- It is an offence to prejudice an investigation, or possible investigation, by tipping off another person information that is likely to be prejudicial.

➡ **Conviction on indictment of these offences is punishable by up to 5 years imprisonment, or a fine, or both.**

Obviously the enforcement of the criminal laws is the responsibility of the law enforcement agencies whether that is the Police or HM Customs & Excise. The **Money Laundering Regulations** are separate laws written for the financial marketplace and are a mandatory obligation for all financial institutions. As such, they require additional administrative requirements. For example, **Regulation 5** provides that all financial businesses must establish and maintain specific policies and procedures to guard against their businesses and the financial system being used for money laundering.

The Regulations cover:

- internal control and communication of policies
- identification procedures
- record keeping
- recognition of suspicious transactions and reporting procedures
- education and training of relevant employees.

➡ **Failure to comply with any of the requirements of the Regulations constitutes an offence punishable by a maximum of 2 years imprisonment, or fine, or both, irrespective of whether money laundering has taken place.**

1. Whether the offence is committed by a Corporate Entity and proved to have been committed with the consent or connivance, or to be attributable to any neglect on the part of, any director, manager, secretary, or officer of the Corporate Entity or any person acting in any such capacity, they as well as the Corporate Entity they as well as the Corporate Entity shall be guilty of that offence and shall be liable to be proceeded against and punished accordingly.

   ➡ **In simple terms, the individual who does not follow laid-down anti-money-laundering procedures will be prosecuted as will his or her employer.**

2. Where the affairs of the Corporate Entity are managed by members, any acts and defaults will be treated as if the member was a director.

3. Where the offence is committed by a partnership or an unincorporated association, the individual, whether he be a partner or person connected with the management or control of the association will be guilty of the offence and shall be liable to be proceeded against and punished accordingly.

Enforcement of the Regulations are now the responsibility of the Financial Services Agency who assess the adherence to the regulations during visits to financial institutions. The Joint Money Laundering Steering Group, an advisory body funded by the financial marketplace, also issue guidelines to financial businesses to help in the fight against money laundering.

Proceeds of Crime (Jersey/Guernsey) Law and what it means (Isle of Man and Gibraltar)

The Jersey and Guernsey Laws were based on the United Kingdom Money Laundering Regulations 1993 with a few minor amendments.

Similarly the Gibraltar and Isle of Man Laws had the same base legislation with local amendments to comply with local requirements.

The current legislation, the obligations and duties of interested bodies are available from the Financial Services/Supervisory Commissions. We have assimilated, analysed and digested the regulations and to summarise:

- No person shall in the course of any financial business carried on by him in the Bailiwick of Jersey/Guernsey form a relationship or carry out a one-off transaction with or for another unless -

  1. he maintains procedures for identification, record keeping, internal reporting and internal control and communication as appropriate for installing money-laundering avoidance procedures and preventing money laundering
  2. he takes appropriate measures from time to time for the purpose of making employees whose duties relate to financial services business aware of the above mentioned procedures, the enactments relating to money laundering and
  3. provides training in connection with money laundering.

  The exception is the individual who does not in the carrying on of a financial business, employ or act in association with any other person.

- Any financial services business carrying on or providing services shall establish and maintain procedures which require that:

  1. they shall produce satisfactory evidence of the identity of the applicant as soon as practicable after first contact is made
  2. they shall discontinue the activity should satisfactory evidence to identity not be obtained
  3. where satisfactory evidence of identity is not obtained the activity may proceed if instructed by a police officer duly authorised for that purpose.

Consequences of ignoring the law

The penalties of non-compliance of the regulations are:

➡ **On conviction, on indictment, to imprisonment not exceeding a term of two years or a fine, or both**

The court may take into account:

• the Guidance Notes on the Prevention of Money Laundering issued by the Financial Services Commission(s) and any other guidance issued, adopted or approved by the Commission(s)

• if no guidance applied to him, any other relevant guidance issued by the body that regulates or is representative of any financial services business carried on by that person

1 Where the offence is committed by a Corporate Entity and proved to have been committed with the consent or connivance, or to be attributable to any neglect on the part of, any director, manager, secretary or officer of the Corporate Entity or any person acting in any such capacity, they as well as the Corporate Entity shall be guilty of that offence and shall be liable to be proceeded against and punished accordingly

➡ **As referred to above, the individual who did not follow laid-down anti-money laundering procedures will be prosecuted, as will their employer.**

2 Where the affairs of the Corporate Entity are managed by members, any acts and defaults will be treated as if the member was a director.

3 Where the offence is committed by a partnership or an unincorporated association, the individual whether he be a partner or person connected with the management or control of the association will be guilty of the offence and shall be liable to be proceeded against and punished accordingly.

In addition the Criminal law has created specific offences in Jersey and Guernsey:

Article 16A – concealing the proceeds of drug trafficking by either a drug trafficker or another (Drug Trafficking Offences (Jersey) Law 1988. Proceeds include cash, gold bullion, coins, jewellery, bills of exchange, promissory notes, insurance policies, securities, precious metals, or stones and works of art.

Article 17 – of the same Law makes it an offence for anyone knowing or suspecting that another person is a drug trafficker to enter an arrangement which facilitates the retention or control of the proceeds of drug trafficking, enables the proceeds to secure funds, or invests the proceeds for the drug trafficker.

Article 17A – of the same Law refers to the acquisition, possession or use of any property which represents in whole or part, directly or indirectly the proceeds of drug trafficking.

The Guernsey Laws are:

- Concealing or transferring the proceeds of Criminal Conduct (CJPCL – Section 38)
- Assisting another person to retain the benefit of criminal conduct (Section 39)
- Acquisition, possession or use of the proceeds of criminal conduct Section 40).

➡ **These offences carry a maximum sentence of 14 years imprisonment if found guilty in both jurisdictions or a fine or both.**

In Jersey there is also an offence under **Article 18A of the Drug Trafficking (Jersey) Law** where it is an offence to fail to disclose information to a Police Officer if that information has arisen in the course of their employment and if they know or suspect that another person is engaged in money laundering. **Article 18B** makes it an offence to disclose information that may prejudice an investigation or to tip off someone by passing on information.

In Guernsey the relevant laws are:

- Tipping Off (Section 41)
- Prejudicing an Investigation (Section 44).

➜ **These offences carry a maximum sentence of 5 years if found guilty in both jurisdictions or a fine or both.**

In Jersey, the law for the prevention of money laundering as included in the **Proceeds of Crime Law 1999** is included in **Section 37, Money Laundering (Jersey) Order 1999**. where the regulations as laid down by the Jersey Financial Services Commission are detailed.

Specific offences within the **Jersey Proceeds of Crime Law** are basically the same as Guernsey with similar sentences if found guilty.

In both jurisdictions, there is legislation in respect of drug trafficking and terrorism that penalises those that aid the criminal in the laundering of their funds.

The Isle of Man and Gibraltar have similar laws with local variations. As all of these laws and regulations are undergoing constant review and change, I would advise obtaining a copy of the local laws and regulations from your Financial Services/Supervision Agency.

Future Laws

The new Financial Services and Markets Bill currently before Parliament may change some of the financial businesses that the regulations apply to. However it is obvious that the Financial Services Authority will be playing a very pro-active role in ensuring compliance to the Law and Regulations.

I have just downloaded the FSA Source Book which details the new rules, subject to Act becoming law, probably during 2001 There are a few changes and it appears that the new rules will refer and operate in parallel to the guidelines issued by the Joint Money Laundering Steering Group. All compliance and money laundering reporting officers should obtain a copy of these rules.

The most interesting rule is the provision for Know Your Client when the client cannot produce identification documents such as a passport, driving licence or utility bills.

The financial business can obtain a letter or statement from a person in a position of responsibility that they know the prospective client, and which tends to show that the client is who they say they are, and confirms their permanent address if they have one. They can then use such evidence to conform to the rules of client identification.

The FSA state that a person in a position of responsibility includes solicitors, doctors, teachers, ministers of religion, hostel managers and social workers.

Wonderful! – the number of reports of suspicious transactions from solicitors are minimal, a doctor currently residing with Her Majesty is the most prolific serial killer the UK has ever known (and laundered inheritances that he stole from his victims), a local hostel manager was recently convicted of allowing the hostel to be used for drug trafficking and more doctors have been struck off for malpractice recently than I can recall. Now, I will apologise to those who may be members of the aforementioned professions and are, like the majority, people of integrity, but when one considers money laundering, it only takes a few financial institutions to ignore the rules and the law, launder dirty money and get caught, to tarnish the whole of the financial industry with the same dirty brush.

Fine – there are people who should be able to invest and cannot produce appropriate identification and their identities need to be verified, but in my opinion, one letter from a person in a position of responsibility is insufficient. It is so easy to forge a simple letter of commendation. I understand that should this rule be abused, the FSA will take appropriate action. Unfortunately it may be a case of closing the gate after the horse has bolted.

In addition, the EC are proposing new anti-money-laundering laws through the European Parliament which will make money laundering an offence if proceeds of crime are handled by solicitors, accountants, estate agents, jewellers, auctioneers, diamond and precious metal dealers, and casino operators. As mentioned previously, the number of suspicious reports from solicitors and accountants are minimal (of 58,000 reports received by NCIS in the period 1995-1998 only 991 came from solicitors).

In the USA, law enforcement groups have advised Congress that the current American laws are inadequate and should be strengthened. They claim that whereas it is illegal to smuggle diamonds and gold it is not illegal to smuggle cash. The only law broken if one smuggles cash is a law of non-reporting to US Customs. The current money laundering laws only cover the attempts to disguise the money as originating from legitimate business as opposed to its origin from crime.

However, the recent confiscation of $60,000 cash by HM Customs & Excise from a racehorse owner en route to the Caribbean because he was unable to confirm the source of the cash shows that a very pro-active stance is being made where large sums of cash are found in passenger's luggage or in their wallets.

Subsequent to the FATF review of the Channel Islands and Isle of Man, a discussion document has been circulated as a joint effort by the three jurisdictions (Jersey, Guernsey, Isle of Man) in respect of Know Your Customer requirements. It is interesting to note that the proposals highlight the weaknesses in certain jurisdictions that, although FATF members, have been recognised by the three Commissions as not equivalent in terms of anti-money-laundering policy. These are Argentina, Aruba, Austria, Brazil, Mexico and Netherlands Antilles. Aruba and the Netherlands Antilles are FATF members as they are seen as part of the Netherlands.

The discussion document calls for:

- documentary evidence of all customers and principals whether introduced locally or from another jurisdiction

- a list of approved jurisdictions agreed by the three Crown Dependencies

- a retrospective client review programme for all clients prior to the introduction of the Proceeds of Crime laws enacted in 1999 and 2000

- reliable introductions of business only to be accepted from regulated entities and resident in 'approved' jurisdictions

- exemptions for certain postal, telephonic and electronic business will be restricted to certain businesses in specified circumstances.

Once the discussion papers are agreed, it is likely the final principles will become law in 2002.

In the UK, a Proceeds of Crime Act is currently before Parliament, which proposes that the Inland Revenue will be able to tax the proceeds of crime.

Hector – how can I help you launder your dirty money with the Inland Revenue?

Do you remember Hector? You know, the bowler-hatted character foisted on the public by the Revenue as a sage and helpful little soul who would help you get your tax affairs in order. Have I got news for you! Despite the patron saint's (Lansky) advice to keep clear of the taxman, our friend Hector, not only moonlighting as a flour grader for Homepride, was apparently caught out laundering money for various criminal organisations – and that may have been the reason for his abrupt dismissal in February 2001.

The criminal gangs have set up or taken over legitimate companies and, following Hector's advice to complete tax returns early and on time, have predicted excessive corporation tax profits for the forthcoming year. They then pay a provisional tax on those forecasted profits and the tax payments are made using the proceeds of crime.

At a later date, the company accountants then claim a tax overpayment as the forecasted profits were not realised. The Inland Revenue agree to refund the overpayment plus interest and the cheque which is made out by them is accepted as clean money anywhere in the world. The Revenue and NCIS are working together to try and identify this latest scheme to launder the proceeds of crime. The problem they have is that NCIS has identified some 938 organised crime gangs in the UK and, as many of these organisations are operated like major multinationals, the true identity of the beneficial owners of 'legitimate' companies may be difficult to substantiate.

I will end this chapter with the findings of the US Senate on 5 February 2001, which state that some of the biggest banks in the USA have failed to prevent billions of dollars from illegal activities such as internet gambling and drug trafficking, being laundered through their accounts. Banks named and shamed include JP Morgan, Citigroup and Bank of America. The Senate claim that the money laundered was facilitated by financial institutions that provided accounts for high-risk off-shore banks. The report said that the US banks were unaware of the 'nature of their clients' because most US banks do not have adequate anti-money-laundering safeguards in place to screen or monitor such banks and the problem is long-standing, widespread and ongoing. The Senate investigation had focused on correspondent banking arrangements by which foreign banks gain access to US banking networks by establishing accounts at banks in North America.

'US correspondent banking provides a significant gateway for rogue foreign banks and their criminal clients to carry on money laundering and other criminal activity in the United States.'

5

Procedures for Prevention

Controls and compliance

Probably the best protection against money laundering is a commitment by the whole organisation to defend itself actively against attack. This principle must be instilled in all members of staff whatever their position and regardless of rank. Frequently, I have seen a cavalier attitude to regulations by senior executives. This attitude is dated and can prove very expensive as the various regulatory bodies are becoming extremely proactive in their stance against those that ignore the rules. Practical policies, procedures and systems need to be implemented.

The vital administrative elements of self-protection are:

- a formal statement from the Board of Directors or senior management team clearly spelling out the organisation's commitment to combat the abuse of its facilities for the purpose of money laundering

- a system of internal control procedures to recognise and deter money laundering by implementation of the following:

  ☑ a designated money laundering officer and deputy responsible for ensuring compliance with internal controls on behalf of the company and with direct access to, but independence from, the Board of Directors

☑ client and counterparty approval procedures and transaction procedures which facilitate the recognition of suspicious transactions and other reportable transactions. Plus the deterrence of fraud, assessment of credit worthiness and ensuring that the client receives the full services offered appropriate to its needs.

☑ record compilation and retention procedures that establish a full transaction audit trail with records that can be admissible as evidence where appropriate

☑ process for the prompt reporting of suspicious transactions to the designated money laundering officer and relevant authorities which complies with both confidentiality and tipping-off laws

☑ an annual self assessment programme to review both the vulnerability of the company and its business lines to both fraud and money laundering and the effectiveness of its money-laundering deterrence procedures

☑ a system to test the procedures implemented by either internal audit, compliance or a competent external source

☑ pre-employment screening systems

☑ appropriate employee training for both new and to refresh existing staff.

Personal Obligations

As mentioned earlier, all employees have obligations under the law and regulations. The main thrust of the legislation is that staff meet their obligations as long as they comply at all times with the approved vigilance policy of their particular financial services business.

Obviously one does not wish to have whistleblowers within the organisation who may go outside to report their suspicions, especially if their reports are ignored. It is essential that all employees have the facility to report any suspicious transaction and that appropriate documentation is available for them to make the report. Verbal reporting should always be confirmed by documentary follow-up. Appropriate procedures should be included in any staff handbook issued and the reporting should be to the delegated reporting officer.

Reporting of incidents procedures

It is important that one does not try to discover the source or reason for the suspicious funds that arrive at your business – that is the job of the law enforcement agencies. The golden rule is – REPORT IT, then leave the processing to the experts.

Key staff should report to either the Reporting Officer or Line Manager (if so required for preliminary investigation in the event of there being other facts that may negate the suspicion). An internal report form should be used and signed by the staff involved with the suspicion and formal reporting.

Acting on information received

The reporting officer, on receipt of the internal report form, needs to assess the information to establish whether it supports the suspicion. The details need to be investigated so that it can be determined whether a report be submitted to the Economic Crime Unit, NCIS, or Financial Crimes Unit.

Most regulatory bodies will expect the Reporting Officer to act honestly, reasonably and to make his or her decisions in good faith. If he or she decides that the information does substantiate a suspicion of laundering, NCIS/FCU should be advised immediately using the standard form prescribed by them. In urgent cases, NCIS/FCU should be advised initially be telephone.

If the reporting officer is uncertain that the information substantiates criminal activity, NCIS /FCU should be advised using the report form as mentioned.

If, in good faith, it is decided that the information does not substantiate the suspicion and no report is made, there is no liability for non-reporting should the judgment be subsequently found to be wrong.

Within the organisation, it is recommended that the vigilance policy include internal reporting procedures so that the appropriate management, whether it be the Compliance Manager, Inspection Department, Group Security Manager or whoever, are informed by the Reporting Officer of suspicious customers/transactions.

A register should be kept, recording:

● date of report
● the author of the report
● the person(s) to whom the report was forwarded
● a reference by which supporting evidence is identifiable.

A separate register should be kept detailing all enquiries made by the FIU or other agencies. This should show:

● the date and nature of the enquiry
● the name and agency of the inquiring officer
● the powers being exercised
● details of the financial services product(s) involved.

It is important to note that the Regulatory Bodies will also require separate reports to be made to them where:

● the financial services business' systems failed to detect a transaction and the matter was reported to the business by an outside source such as NCIS/FCU

● the transaction may present a significant risk to the reputation of the financial centre and/or the business

- it is suspected that a staff member of the financial service business is involved

- a staff member of the financial service business has been dismissed for serious control breaches.

As mentioned, the regulations require record keeping so that an audit trail is maintained so that, in the event of an investigation, the document/transaction sequence can be followed.

These records must be kept to certain prescribed Time Limits, and, depending on whether transactions or electronic transfers, certain details. A full list of these requirements can be obtained from the regulatory body (usually available on CD-Rom or floppy disk). Usually it is required that they be kept in readily retrievable form, so do not pack them away in a dusty storeroom so that it takes five years to find them. If kept on computer, the condition of the records should be examined periodically to ensure they are in good condition. Disaster recovery procedures should also be regularly monitored.

Self-assessment programme

This should be completed annually to review any vulnerabilities to money laundering, fraud and the effectiveness of the deterrence procedures.

A report should be completed documenting the work performed, who carried it out, how it was controlled and supervised, together with findings, conclusions and recommendations.

Management should be advised whether the internal procedures and statutory obligations have been properly completed.

The following questions should be answered:

- what have been the changes to our risk profile?
- what changes have their been to money laundering methods?
- do our money laundering deterrence procedures suit our risk profile?

- to what extent and in what manner are they being adhered to?
- how do they interact with other policies, controls and statutory requirements of the business?

Independent Testing

Internal Audit or Compliance should implement an annual independent test of the effectiveness of the money laundering deterrence procedures which should include:

- interview of employees handling transactions and supervisors to determine their knowledge and compliance with the procedures

- sampling types of transactions with a review of associated transactions, record retention documentation and suspicious transaction referral reports

- testing the reasonableness and validity of any exemptions granted to clients

- testing the record keeping system set up in 'Record Retention'. Any deficiencies should be reported to the appropriate manager with a request for corrective action and a deadline for implementation.

Should staffing levels prohibit such testing consideration should be given to using an external contractor.

Pre-employment screening and employee training

Recent studies show that the number of job applications that contain false information are as high as 25%. In the United Kingdom it is a criminal offence to gain employment by false references and qualifications. The subject of pre-employment screening can easily be the subject of a separate book and we have mentioned this subject in Chapter Three. Obviously, it is important that all prospective employees are vetted to ensure that the financial business does not suffer the consequences of employing the dishonest. With the law and its obligations, the last thing needed is the employment of an individual who may be vulnerable to dishonesty, especially bribery. Appropriate vetting procedures for new employees and appropriate anti-money-laundering training programmes for both new and existing employees are all essential.

We recommend that a pre-employment screening programme be implemented if not in place. Existing programmes should be evaluated and where appropriate improved to prevent the rotten apple slipping through the door.

Conclusion

I hope that you have enjoyed this small book, but even so, no doubt the problems of money laundering will continue. It is important to remember the statement at the beginning of this book – there is no dirty money, only dirty people Without the criminal and his dishonest banker, accountant, insurance man, and/or lawyer, there are no proceeds of crime to convert to what appears to be legitimate assets. Most of the money-laundering cases in this book and other publications are the result of either internal dishonesty or lack of diligence. How often when a case hits the proverbial fan does the financial institution claim that they thought that the institution that transferred the money to them had completed proper verification?

- Can you be sure their procedures are as good as yours?

- Even though they are on the FATF approved list, are you sure about them?

The case now hitting the press in respect of the Abacha family stealing millions of pounds of Nigerian Government money highlights funds being deposited and transferred between British and European banks where it appears that due diligence may have gone out of the window at many well established international banks. The Swiss are blaming London, London is blaming Luxembourg, no doubt someone, somewhere will decide that it's all due to Mickey Mouse, Enid Blyton and Hans Christian Anderson. In March 2001, the FSA was quoted as being 'disappointed' that some £89million of Sani Abacha's ill-gotten gains had been laundered through banks in London and demands were made for a considerable tightening of vetting controls. This is a tale that will run and run.

As this book goes to print some of the world's leading banks (including Citibank) have announced new guidelines for the prevention of money laundering (The Wolfsberg Principles), yet a recent investigation into Russian funds laundered in the USA has revealed that Citibank's anti-money laundering procedures in the USA were allegedly extremely poor with Russian funds being laundered through Delaware-registered shell companies.

The Joint Money Laundering Steering Group announced a conference in February 2001, when they introduced new guidelines in line with the new FSA regulations. Even HM Queen Elizabeth II, at the State Opening of Parliament (6 December 2000), announced proposed Proceeds of Crime legislation to recover the assets of criminals and organised crime, and a Parliamentary committee has requested lawyers and accountants to attend and be interviewed about money laundering issues and lack of reporting of suspicious transactions. So, everyone is jumping on the proverbial bandwagon. However, being cynical, one has to ask whether the new laws, controls and regulations will go far enough and institutions will continue to pay lip service to the regulations, or will cybermoney laundering escape and bypass these laws.

The French parliament's action force into money laundering has now attacked the Swiss, calling them 'a predator of world finance waging a sham war against money laundering'. The French allege that the number of money laundering cases reported by financial instituitions in 1999-2000 was derisory, with the 372 banks in Switzerland identifying only 313 suspicious transaction reports. The Swiss have rejected these findings, claiming that, whereas the French banks reported some 1,655 suspicious transactions, the percentage acted upon and prosecuted in Switzerland was higher with 65.4% of cases being acted upon. In France, the percentage was only 7%. The French investigators plan reports on money laundering in the United Kingdom, the Channel Islands and Gibraltar.

No doubt, there is a forum for debate as to whether Governments should do more than leave the onus of responsibility on the financial businesses, especially when one looks at the cost of computer control systems to identify those suspicious wire transfers. Perhaps a more proactive stance is called for with mandatory reporting of all transactions above a defined level, and the criminal intelligence organisations implementing appropriate computer based interrogation programmes to examine these transactions.

To close, the millions I will make from this book, which in a perverse way are proceeds of crime (no you cannot have a refund!), will not go offshore but go to help the important cancer research at The Royal Free Hospital in London in recognition of the help they have given to my wife and others.

Bob Blunden
March 2001

Recommended Reading

The Laundrymen, Jeffrey Robinson, Simon and Schuster, UK 1994

A Full Service Bank, James Ring Adams and Douglas Franz, Simon and Schuster, New York, 1992

Evil Money, Rachel Ehrenfeld, HarperCollins, New York, 1992

The Dragon Syndicates, Martin Booth, Doubleday/Bantam Books, UK, 1999

Review to Identify Non-Cooperative Countries or Territories, 22 June 2000, Financial Action Task Force on Money Laundering

Altavista live – news web site http://live.altavista.com

Jersey Financial Services Commission Guidance Notes/Regulations/Law

Guernsey Financial Services Commission Guidance Notes/Regulations/Law

Isle of Man Supervision Commission Guidance Notes/Regulations/Law

Gibraltar Financial Service Commission Guidance Notes/ Regulations/Law

Guidance Notes for the Financial Sector – Joint Money Laundering Steering Group

The Merger, Jeffrey Robinson, Simon and Schuster, UK , 1999

www.offshore-net.com/newshot/offshorescam

Index